# Social Work Practice
# for Social Justice

# Social Work Practice for Social Justice

## CULTURAL COMPETENCE IN ACTION

**BETTY GARCIA**     **DOROTHY VAN SOEST**

COUNCIL ON SOCIAL WORK EDUCATION
ALEXANDRIA, VIRGINIA

**Library of Congress Cataloging-in-Publication Data**

Garcia, Betty, 1943–

  Social work practice for social justice : cultural competence in action / Betty Garcia and Dorothy Van Soest.

      p. cm.

   Includes bibliographical references and index.

   ISBN 0-87293-124-2 (alk. paper)

  1. Social service—United States.   2. Social justice—United States.
3. Social work with minorities—United States.   I. Van Soest, Dorothy.
II. Title.

   HV91.G327 2006
   361.301—dc22

                                                                    2006007339

ISBN 0-87293-124-2

Printed in the United States of America on acid-free paper that meets the American National Standards Institute Z39-48 Standard.
Council on Social Work Education, Inc.

1725 Duke Street, Suite 500
Alexandria, VA 22314-3457
www.cswe.org

# Contents

# Preface

This volume is intended as a companion text to our earlier work, *Diversity Education for Social Justice: Mastering Teaching Skills*. That work was developed for faculty to identify the multitude of dimensions that must be mastered for effective teaching of social justice and diversity content. Those dimensions include intellectual knowledge of concepts related to racism and theoretical orientations that encompass political, economic, and social factors. Equally important, that text focused on the psychological and emotional work and preparedness that is a major component of diversity learning. This text derives its key concepts and frameworks from that work, while orienting the discussion to student learning and experiences.

As a student text, this work is meant to engage students and stimulate learning about racism and social justice, curiosity about diverse others, and self-awareness. With that in mind we focused on clearly and succinctly presenting fundamental and vitally significant concepts that define and elaborate on racism and institutional qualities, oppression, classism, social justice, and social identity. We firmly believe that as educators our roles are to open doors to self-initiated learning and to support the journey that many of you have already started.

Through this work, which is intended for both undergraduate and graduate courses, we hope to reach future generations of social work professionals. This book came about as a result of considerable support and invaluable commentary and feedback from various sources. We expect that it is most effective if all the exercises are done in the order in which they are developed. Students can read these on their own, some can be done in the classroom or as assignments, and others can be used as a focus of classroom discussion.

Some formative faculty discussions on teaching this content that facilitated critical thinking on these topics were supported by Joseph Regan, former dean at Simmons College in Boston. His efforts recognized the

importance of this content in social work education and the role of administration in promoting its visibility in the curriculum. The Council on
Publications at the Council on Social Work Education staff was invaluable in
raising issues regarding enhancing the usability of a work like this for
undergraduate and graduate students. Their insights and patience in the
production of this work are greatly appreciated. We also thank the graduate
students at California State University, Fresno, who reviewed part of the
manuscript and offered insightful and critical thinking. They are Lovejit
Bahia, Josie Burnias, Rohina Fazil, Estella Gonzalez, Marshunda Harding,
Armida Hernandez, Renee Hoover, Thomas Jones, Dale Lacy, Melissa Mitchell,
Felicity Moreno, Laura Orozco, Veronica Orozco, Robert Quintero, Kimberly
Trejo, Paige Turner Sambueso, Ernesto Santillan, Pamela Young, and Kia
Vang.

Betty Garcia & Dorothy Van Soest
*Summer 2006*

# List of Reflection Exercises, Classroom Exercises, Assignments, Figures, Charts, and Tables

## Reflection Exercises

(continued)

## Reflection Exercises (continued)

## Classroom Exercises

## Assignment

## Figures

## Charts

## Table

# Chapter One
# The Foundation:
# Understanding Social Justice

A major premise of this book is that a commitment to promoting social justice for diverse individuals and populations is the foundation for culturally competent social work practice. This requirement is supported by the mandates that social workers challenge social injustice and promote social and economic justice, as stated in the National Association of Social Workers Code of Ethics (NASW, 1996), the *International Declaration of Ethical Principles of Social Work* of the International Federation of Social Workers (IFSW, 1994), and the *Educational Policy and Accreditation Standards* of the Council on Social Work Education (CSWE, 2001).

The major purpose of this book is to help prepare professional social workers to transform oppressive and unjust systems into nonoppressive and just alternatives (Gil, 1998). It is based on a vision that the social work profession can become firmly and unequivocally committed to eliminating oppression and promoting social justice. In an essay, entitled "Failure to Quit," historian Howard Zinn (1997) provides hope for the work that lies ahead if this vision is to be realized:

> I can understand pessimism, but I don't believe in it. It's not simply a matter of faith, but of historical evidence. Not overwhelming evidence, just enough to give hope, because for hope we don't need certainty, only possibility. Which is all history can offer us. When I hear so often that there is little hope for change from the present generation of young people, I think back to the despair [about the possibilities for change in the United States at the beginning of the 1960s]. Yet, it was on the first of February in that first year of the new decade that four black students from North Carolina A&T College sat down at a "white" lunch counter in Greensboro, refused to

**1**

move, and were arrested. In two weeks, sit-ins had spread to fifteen cities in five Southern states. By the year's end, 50,000 people had participated in demonstrations in a hundred cities, and 3,600 had been put in jail. That was the start of the civil rights movement, which became an anti-war movement, a women's movement, a cultural upheaval, and in its course hundreds of thousands, no millions, of people became committed for a short time, or for a lifetime. It was unprecedented, unpredicted, and for at least fifteen years, uncontrollable. It would shake the country and startle the world, with consequences we are hardly aware of today . . .

There is no such uproar today. There is an uncertain mixture of silence and commotion . . . but there is more than silence. . . . There are thousands of local groups around the country—many more than existed in the Sixties—devoted to struggling for tenants' rights or women's rights or environmental protection . . . or to take care of the hungry and the homeless, or those in need of health care. There are now tens of thousands of professionals . . . who bring unorthodox ideas and humane values into courtrooms, classrooms, and hospitals. . . . History does not start anew with each decade. The roots of one era branch and flower in subsequent eras. Human beings, writings, invisible transmitters of all kinds, carry messages across the generations. I try to be pessimistic, to keep up with some of my friends. But I think back over the decades, and look around. And then, it seems to me that the future is not certain, but it is possible. (pp. 656–661)

This chapter challenges you to ask critical questions and to be open to examine and, if needed, modify or change your perspective about justice to develop as a culturally competent professional. It provides foundation information aimed at helping increase understanding of the social justice vision for social work. The first section starts with a brief discussion of social justice definitions. In the second section, we ask you to start with yourself by bringing to light and examining your own perspective on social justice. We then provide brief descriptions of prevalent social justice theories, including normative mainstream philosophical perspectives; the racial contract that integrates diversity and oppression with social justice theory; and the human rights perspective that builds on and broadens the racial contract to emphasize solutions. The social justice perspectives provide signposts against which you can analyze your own personal theory of justice and examine the practice implications.

# Defining Social Justice

While the professional mandates that social workers promote social justice and challenge social injustice are clear (CSWE, 2001; IFSW, 1994; NASW, 1996), there is no specific definition of social justice. Thus, social workers face the immediate challenge of understanding what social justice and social injustice mean. Social justice as an idea has historically been highly contested, and it has taken on various meanings over time. As is seen later in this chapter, one's perspective on social justice is often related to one's own social position in society. The problem with that, as Reisch (2002) points out, is that people end up marching under the banner of social justice while promoting radically different ideas of what it is; for example, "liberals and conservatives, religious fundamentalists, and radical secularists all regard their causes as socially just" (p. 343), and it is not uncommon for some people to claim to be for social justice while others accuse them of not being for social justice.

Several related definitions in the social work literature provide a guide for thinking about what social justice is, even though there is not one universally accepted definition. The *Encyclopedia of Social Work* (Flynn, 1995) defines social justice as the embodiment of fairness (reasonable treatment), equity (similar situations dealt with similarly), and equality in the distribution of societal resources. *The Social Work Dictionary* (Barker, 2003) defines social justice as "An ideal condition in which all members of a society have the same basic rights, protection, opportunities, obligations, and social benefits. Implicit in this concept is the notion that historical inequalities should be acknowledged and remedied through specific measures. As a key social work value, social justice entails advocacy to confront discrimination, oppression, and institutional inequities" (pp. 404–405). Doman Lum (personal communication, May 9, 2005) provides definitions of both social justice and economic justice:

> Social justice governs how social institutions deal fairly or justly with the social needs of people as far as opening access to what is good for individuals and groups. It also secures social rights and benefits in terms of social provisions of well-being such as nutrition, housing, employment, education, and health care. Social justice also addresses historical and current forms of oppression and seeks legal and societal means to correct such abuses and

establish an equal playing field for all regardless of ethnicity, gender, sexual orientation, social and economic class, age, and other related factors.

Economic justice encompasses moral principles of how to design economic institutions so that a person can earn a living, enter into social and economic contracts (monetary agreements to buy a car, house; obtain assets, e.g., stocks), exchange goods and services in order to produce an independent material foundation for economic sustenance. It also ensures education and employment to nurture people in learning and career development and, when they are unable to provide for themselves, economic justice fosters temporary welfare assistance until a person can function in a work environment.

In this chapter, three types of social justice are recognized—distributive, legal, and commutative. Wakefield (1988) favors distributive justice as the organizing value of social work, a position that is taken in this chapter as well. However, if we are to connect the dots between social work's traditional notion that citizens have a right to have their needs met and issues of multiculturalism, cultural competence, and oppression—a main contention of this book—then the distributive paradigm is not sufficient to encapsulate the complexities of injustice (Young, 1990). The concept of social justice needs to be about more than the distribution of income and other goods and services; "a concept of justice should begin with the concepts of domination and oppression" and should seek institutional remedies for "cultural sources of oppression, the manifestations of which are seen in racism, sexism, homophobia, ableism, etc." (van Wormer, 2004, p. 12). *The Racial Contract* (Mills, 1997), discussed at length later in this chapter, integrates issues of social justice with cultural diversity and the impact of oppression on historically disadvantaged people.

# Beginning With Awareness, Reflection, and Critical Thinking

To understand what the mandate to promote social and economic justice means, it is important to start with oneself. This section begins by asking you about your values and beliefs about social justice and where those values and beliefs originated.

The following reflection exercises encourage you to look at your own answers to the questions: Is life fair? If so, why? If not, why not? If life is fair, why do you consider it to be fair? The questions are intended to help you to engage conscientiously in a process of reflection and critical thinking about the implications of your current perspective.

**REFLECTION EXERCISE 1.1  FAIRNESS AND JUSTICE**

Throughout our lives, often beginning at a young age, we hear expressions such as: "That's not fair!" "You're not playing fair!" and "Life is not fair!" Such expressions usually coincide with disappointment or when something bad happens to us or to someone we care about. The expression is perhaps a manifestation of a belief that life is, indeed, not fair, at least not to us at that moment. Underlying any expression about fairness is a social justice perspective, as each of us has one whether or not we know what it is.

As we were growing up, we received many messages about fairness and justice. Take a few minutes to recall some of those messages. You may remember a particular situation in which you learned a lesson about what was fair or unfair, just or unjust. What did you learn from the situation? What did the adults around you (parents, other caretakers, teachers) teach you about fairness? How do you carry those messages with you today? Which ones do you hold on to? Which ones have you discarded?

**REFLECTION EXERCISE 1.2  RIGHT AND PRIVILEGES***

Take some time to write your responses to the following questions:

1. What are rights? What do people have a right to (i.e., what do people deserve just because they're human beings)?

2. What are privileges (i.e., what do people deserve because they have earned it)?

## RIGHT AND PRIVILEGES (continued)

3. Is it fair to take (e.g., through taxes) from one group and give to another group? When is it fair and when is it not fair? Does it have to with rights or privileges? When is it a form of justice and when is it an infringement on people's freedom?

4. If there is a situation in which the goods and services produced are inadequate to satisfy everyone's desire for them, on what basis or according to what principles can these goods and services be distributed justly? For example, if you believe that everyone has a right to food but there is an inadequate supply, how do you distribute it? If you believe that having food is a privilege, then what do people have to do to earn it? And what should be done when people who have not earned it get it and those who earn it do not get it?

5. If there is a situation in which the goods and services produced are adequate to satisfy everyone's desire for them, on what basis or according to what principles can they be distributed justly?

### Reflection and Discussion

Now take a moment to read your responses and reflect on them. What, if any, themes do you see? Do you believe that life is just (fair), and, if so, what does justice mean based on your responses? Do you believe life is unjust (unfair)? Where do your beliefs come from? How comfortable are you with them? In a small group or in pairs, discuss each question and how you think you came to the position that you took.

---

*This exercise was adapted from Van Soest, 2003, pp. 349–350.

The following classroom discussion exercises are intended to stimulate further awareness of your own perspective on social justice and the application of your perspective to specific situations. A key point is the importance of understanding how you use the term *justice* and consider guiding principles that you use to make decisions about what justice is in particular situations.

## Classroom Exercise 1.1  Demands*

Read the scenario and then discuss the questions that follow.

Recently the workers at a major university went on strike to call attention to their demands. One of the demands was that all staff with salaries up to $60,000 should get an across-the-board salary increase of $400 per month.

1. In your opinion, is the workers' demand a *just* one? Do you think it is a fair demand? Why?

2. Should the amount of increase be based on the amount of time a person has worked at the university (e.g., a person who just started work a month ago versus a person who has worked there for 10 years)?

3. Is it fair (just) that a worker making $59,000 would get the same amount as a worker who is only making $15,000 a year?

4. Should the cutoff point be $60,000? Why not set it at $30,000? On what basis would you make such a decision?

5. Would it be fair (just) to demand the salary increase only for workers earning salaries in the bottom quartile? Explain why.

6. As you think about your responses to the above questions, what beliefs or principles did you use to arrive at your position?

---

*This exercise was adapted from Van Soest, 2003, pp. 350–351.

## Classroom Exercise 1.2  Fair Distribution

Provide enough of some kind of food so that every person could have a generous portion (e.g., crackers, fruit slices, peanuts, small candies). Divide the class into small discussion groups. Each group must decide how to distribute the food to the class in a fair and just way. Each

*Fair Distribution (continued)*

group will present its distribution plan to the whole class. After each group has presented its plan, discuss the following questions:

1. What distribution system did each group select (e.g., that every-one should get an *equal* amount; that distribution should be based on *need* by determining who hasn't eaten breakfast or lunch yet; that distribution should be based on *merit*)?

2. Which system would you consider to be most fair? Most just?

3. Might there be a situation when one system would be more fair and just than it would be in another situation? On what basis do you make such a distinction?

If the class can agree on which distribution system is most fair (just), distribute the food based on that system. Whether or not the class can agree on a system, discuss the following questions:

1. Do you think that there is one distribution system that social work as a profession should conform to?

2. If so, what should that system be? Would it apply to all situa-tions? When might a different system be more fair (just)?

3. Might having more than one system be congruent and consistent with social work values?

4. What are the implications of these strategies discussed in class for real-life situations involving decisions about distribution of resources?

# Social Justice Theory

The intent of the above exercises was to encourage you to struggle with the question of justice. What is it? Is justice *equality*? Is justice having *freedom*? Does justice mean meeting *needs?* If so, how do we distinguish between what are *needs* and what are *privileges?* These and many other questions point to the complexities involved in determining what is just and fair. Whether aware of it or not, each of us believes in certain principles and theories of what justice is. And, as Figure 1.1 illustrates, one's perspective on what is just and fair is often related to one's own social position in society. The previous awareness section was intended to illustrate the importance of rigor in one's thinking about what social justice means and how to go about taking social work's social justice mandate seriously.

### FIGURE 1.1 SOCIAL JUSTICE PERSPECTIVES

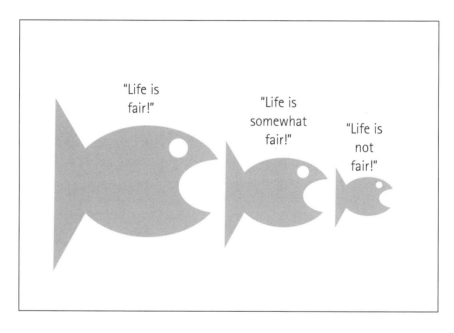

Social justice is far more complicated than it sometimes seems when people are engaged in intense discussion about a situation they consider as unfair. There seems to be a misperception among social workers that everyone means the same thing when they use the term *social justice*. This misperception can lead to finger-pointing, with some people claiming to be *for* social justice while others accuse them of *not* being for social justice. Critical thinking requires the development of a knowledge base of frameworks that provide a foundation for examining and challenging one's personal perspectives; wrestling with the issue of which social justice perspectives and principles are coherent and congruent with social work values; and applying that understanding to effective strategies for promoting justice and fairness on individual, community, organizational, and societal levels.

What follows is a brief review of some principles and contemporary social justice theories that are prevalent in the literature, with a focus on distributive justice. It is hoped that the complexities of issues related to social justice and the need for critical thinking and continuous knowledge development as professionals will be apparent from this overview.

## Types of Social Justice

In discussions about social justice, it is important to recognize that conceptually there are different types of social justice—distributive, legal, and commutative—and there are different understandings of what these types represent. The types of social justice are grounded in the social contract tradition that has prevailed among political philosophers, including Hobbes, Locke, Kant, Rousseau, John Rawls, and Robert Nozick. Considerations about what society owes the individual involve reflecting on distributive justice. When considering what the individual owes to society, we are talking about legal justice. When considering what individuals owe to each other, we are talking about commutative justice. The types of justice are illustrated in Figure 1.2.

**FIGURE 1.2  TYPES OF JUSTICE**

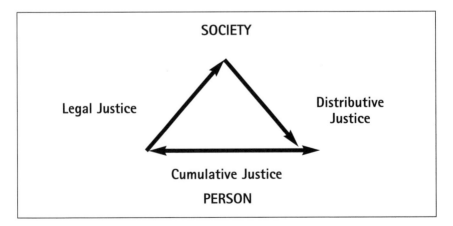

While social work is concerned about all of these types of social justice, the focus of this chapter is on distributive justice. This is because distributive justice, which involves the ways in which resources are allocated in society, is closely linked to the social work mission of promoting social and economic justice. The resources that concern social workers include a broad range of goods and services, from economic assistance to access to counseling and therapy. Wakefield (1988) argues that the organizing value of social work is distributive justice and that Rawls (1971) provides the most coherent framework for our profession. Rawls's perspective is presented later. Beverly and McSweeney's (1987) definition of justice for social work emphasizes its distributive quality as well: "Justice . . . means fairness in the relationships between people as these related to the possession and/or acquisition of resources based on some kind of valid claim to a share of those resources . . . the justice or injustice of a particular policy or situation is determined by looking at the fairness of the distribution of resources in relation to the claims or demands made for those resources" (p. 5). For social workers, the distribution of goods other than political or economic resources, such as health services, education, and leisure, is within the realm of social justice. To begin thinking about distributive justice, do the exercise below.

**REFLECTION EXERCISE 1.3   FAIR DISTRIBUTION**

Read the following scenario and then reflect on the questions that follow.

If you imagine that there are 25 people in the world and there are 25 apples cut into quarters, or 100 slices, this is how those slices would be distributed into portions proportionate to the way food is distributed to people worldwide:

- •Six people would receive nothing or crumbs.
- •Seven people would receive one slice each.
- •Six people would receive three slices each.
- •Five people would receive 10 slices each.
- •One person would receive 25 slices.

**FAIR DISTRIBUTION (continued)**

Write your reactions to the following questions before engaging in classroom discussion.

1. Is this worldwide distribution of food just or unjust?

2. Can you think of any situation or condition in which this kind of disparity might be just?

3. What principles or kinds of situations might be used to conclude that such disparities are, in fact, just?

While most people might quickly conclude from Reflection Exercise 1.3 that the disparities in the way the world eats are clearly unjust, others might consider whether their justness or unjustness could depend on certain qualifying conditions, and still others might even say they are actually just. How do we account for such different conclusions among social workers as well as among others? The following overview of theories of distributive justice illustrates how each might judge the justness of disparities of distribution differently.

Five competing contemporary theories of distributive justice illustrate the varied lenses through which justice is viewed and determined. The first three perspectives to be presented—utilitarian (see Hare, 1992; Sidgwick, 1966), libertarian (Nozick, 1974), and egalitarian (Rawls, 1971)—are *prescriptive* rather than descriptive in that they present a case for what social justice *should* be or distinct ways that social justice *should* be defined. The fourth conceptual perspective, the racial contract (Mills, 1997), differs in that it is *descriptive* rather than prescriptive in that it describes what is. The racial contract perspective addresses the situation *as it is now*, what the state of our society and the world is in relation to achieving any semblance of social justice. The fifth view is a human rights perspective that is gaining ground because of its assumptions about social justice and basic rights. Each of these five conceptual perspectives is briefly discussed below. Together, they provide a theoretical framework from which to examine and critically analyze one's own perspectives.

## Utilitarian Perspective

The major proponent of the utilitarian perspective of social justice is John Stuart Mill (Sterba, 1985). The key question from this perspective is: What distribution of goods, what principles of justice, what ascriptions of rights are such that their acceptance serves the general interest? Justice is arrived at by weighing relative benefits and harms and determining what maximizes the greatest good for the greatest number of people. Thus, from a utilitarian perspective, it may be determined that social justice exists even if some people have no rights met and others have all their rights met, as long as it is determined that it is for the common good. Utilitarian justice tends to produce a distribution of goods and services similar to a bell curve, with most people getting their needs met and a small percentage getting none of their needs met, while another small percentage gets more than what they need (see Figure 1.3).

**FIGURE 1.3   UTILITARIAN PERSPECTIVE OF SOCIAL JUSTICE**

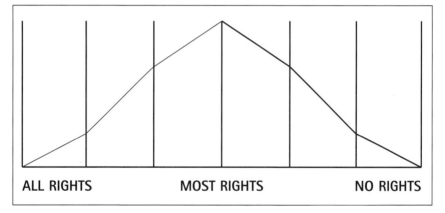

| ALL RIGHTS | MOST RIGHTS | NO RIGHTS |

The definition of the common good, which is open to varied viewpoints, determines whether one believes a situation is just. For example, some people believe that it is not for the common good if some people are provided for when they can provide for themselves. On the other hand, others may argue that when some groups are not provided for, the common good is not served because there may be unrest or because it harms us all morally, as individuals and as a society.

Another example is how policy-makers holding to the utilitarian perspective might come up with very different positions on how to distribute resources, depending on their definition of the common good. When faced with the question of whether society's resources should go into education or the military, the definition of the common good determines one's position. If the common good is seen as primarily to protect the country's citizens from external attack by another nation, then policies would perhaps be developed that channeled resources into the military at the expense of education. If the common good, on the other hand, is seen as an educated citizenry, then policies would be developed that channeled resources into education first, perhaps at the expense of the military. If the common good is defined as an educated citizenry *and* a protected citizenry, then policies would seek to divide resources between education and the military.

## Libertarian Perspective

In contrast to the utilitarian perspective, the libertarian position advanced by Robert Nozick (1974) is based on the principle that the distribution of resources occurs by means of a natural and social lottery. This translates into a position of noninterference with the natural order of things.

Distribution, therefore, is naturally uneven. This theory is considered to be amoral and based on a description of the social contract as occurring naturally. That is to say, there are laws of nature that regulate distribution. For example, some people are born with higher intellectual capacities than others, some people get lucky in relation to money and others don't, some people are born into rich cultures and some into poor cultures, and so on. The libertarian view of this natural distribution is seen as inherently fair in that it is not based on morality but rather on chance or the natural order of things.

According to the libertarian perspective, people hold certain rights by entitlement. What they have, they are entitled to by virtue of the fact that they have it. Thus, justice consists in the widest possible latitude of freedom from coercion in what people accumulate and what, how, and when they dispose of it. This view would suggest, for example, that those opposed to taxation should not be coerced into compliance. On the other hand, tax dollars going to the military may be acceptable because the military may be seen as protecting this fundamental freedom.

This perspective sees a rebalancing of justice as occurring naturally over time. Thus, when we notice that people are oppressed or denied resources, we are only seeing a "snapshot" in time rather than attending to contextual, long-term factors. From this historical perspective, if we were to look over time, we might see that this oppressed group was the oppressor in the past and/or may become the oppressor in the future. Also, from this perspective, value is placed on giving to others, and charity is considered a virtue. However, in a just society each person has the freedom to determine how much, to whom, and when to give. No institution or person should interfere with that basic freedom or with the natural order of things.

## Egalitarian Perspective

Egalitarian theory, based on Locke's theory of the social contract and developed by John Rawls (1971), maintains that if we were to design a just society, we would need to do so under a veil of ignorance. What this means is that those who attempt to design a just society would not know in advance what their position in that society would be and thus would have a stake in avoiding extreme inequalities at the outset. For example, since you might be born into society with severe developmental disabilities, you would want to ensure that you would have access to the resources needed for your care and growth. Or, since you might be born into a very poor family, you would want to ensure that there was a distribution system that would help you and your family.

In a just society designed from an egalitarian perspective, two principles would not  accept inequalities to achieve a greater common good (utilitarianism) or to maintain individual freedom (libertarianism). The first principle requires that basic liberties must be equal, because citizens of a just society have the same basic rights to freedom, to fair equality of opportunity, to access to goods and services, and to self-respect. Thus, if you were born as a poor person into this just society, you would have liberties that are equal to those of the richest person in the society. The second principle asserts that, although the actual distribution of income and wealth need not be equal, any inequalities in power, wealth, and other resources must not exist *unless* they work to the absolute benefit of the worst-off members of society. For example, if you were born with serious medical conditions, under this principle you might receive more resources in your early years than are provided to others because you would need them more to have equal opportunity in life. Thus, there would be an inequality in distribution of educational services, but it would work to the absolute benefit of you as one of the worst-off members of society.

From an egalitarian perspective, in contrast to the libertarian view, redistribution of resources is a moral obligation. The unmet needs that should be redressed first should be of those who are most in need. This means that, to provide genuine equality of opportunity, society must give more attention to those with fewer native assets and to those born into less favorable social positions. For example, according to egalitarian principles, greater resources might be spent on the education of the less rather than the more intelligent students in our schools, at least in their earlier years, to ensure equality of opportunity in life.

# The Racial Contract

In his book, *The Racial Contract* (1997), Charles C. W. Mills provides a way of connecting the previous perspectives about what *should* be with what *is* in terms of the reality of the injustices that are so prevalent in our society and world. Mills's perspective is based on the social contract tradition that is also central to the other three contemporary social justice theories.

However, from this perspective, the notion of the social contract as the basis of Western democratic societies is in fact a myth; the actual (i.e., in practice) basis of Western societies is a racial contract. The basic difference between Mills's perspective of social justice and the first three is that the particular social contract to which Mills refers is not a contract among everybody (as in "we the people"), but rather is a contract only between people who count and have social position, that is, the people who are considered to be *people*, as in "we the White, people" (who are upper class).

Utilitarians, libertarians, and egalitarians use the social contract as a *normative* tool, that is, as an *ideal* social contract that explains how a just society, ruled by a moral government, *should* be formed and regulated by a defensible moral code. Mills's (1997) use of the social contract is different. He uses it not merely normatively, but *descriptively*, to explain the *actual* genesis of a society, a people's moral psychology, and how a government functions.

According to the racial contract, it is crucial to understand what the original and continuing social contract actually was and is today, so that we can correct for it in constructing the ideal contract toward which social work can then strive.

According to Mills, the social contract has always consisted of formal and informal agreements between the members of one subset of individuals who are designated as White (dominant) and who are, by implication, seen as legitimate in comparison to other groups. The remaining subset of individuals, who are designated as "non-White" and of a different and inferior moral status of subpersons, is not a participatory, consenting party to the contract—that is, subjects acting on the agreement—but rather the objects being acted upon. Mills's main point is that the general purpose of the social contract, in reality, has always been the differential and biased privileging of Whites in relation to non-Whites as a group. From the beginning then, "race" is not an "afterthought" or a "deviation" from ostensibly race-neutral Western ideals of the social contract, but rather a core element of those ideals.

The racial contract has strong support as a historical fact. Mills describes specific derivative contracts designed for different modes of exploitation of international resources and peoples, all for the benefit of Europe. For example, the slavery contract, colonial contract, and expropriation contract granted Europeans absolute dominion over all territories of the world, not by virtue of conquering them, but as a right acquired simply by "discovery." In sum, the racial contract presents an argument that society is currently unjust, and that it is unjust because people who are considered to be non-White have always been excluded from the social contract that determines distribution of resources.

## Human Rights Perspective

From a human rights perspective, social justice "encompasses satisfaction of basic human needs and the equitable sharing of material resources" (United Nations, 1992, p.16). Human rights are seen as basic rights that are inherent in our nature, and without them we could not live as human beings because they are integral to a life with dignity and respect. Human rights are universal and a basic entitlement, without discrimination, for *all*, regardless of race, gender, or class. This approach represents a shift from a "defensive stance against oppression to an affirmation of the right to satisfaction of material and non-material human needs and equitable participation in the production and distribution of resources" (United Nations, 1992, p. 6).

Basic rights include the assurance of freedom, certainty of social justice, and assurance of the social and international order needed to realize one's rights and freedoms. They include the right to develop and exercise our human capabilities, such as intelligence, talents, and conscience. They promote dignity in people's lives. Human rights include much of what is discussed in the capabilities approach (Nussbaum, 2000, 2001), such as the right to life, bodily health, bodily integrity (i.e., freedom to move where one chooses), imagination and thought, emotions (e.g., forming attachments and not having emotional development limited by fear and anxiety), affiliation, and play and control over one's physical and social environment. From this perspective, the presence of human rights in individuals' lives promotes quality of life. Figure 1.4 provides a short summary of the basic instruments concerning human rights, with the dates when they were adopted by the United Nations General Assembly. The list illustrates the comprehensive nature of the human rights perspective.

**FIGURE 1.4**
## SUMMARY OF HUMAN RIGHTS INSTRUMENTS ADOPTED BY THE UNITED NATIONS.*

### INSTRUMENTS PROVIDING GENERAL PROTECTION

The Universal Declaration of Human Rights (1948)
The Covenants on Human Rights (1966)

**The International Covenant on Civil and Political Rights**
- Right to life, liberty, and security
- Right not to be subjected to torture and cruel, inhuman, or degrading treatment or punishment
- Prohibition of slavery
- Right not to be detained arbitrarily
- Rights to freedom of expression, religion, assembly, and association, including trade union membership
- Right to freedom of movement and residence

- Right to vote through universal suffrage
- Right to a fair trial
- Rights of minorities to protection

**The International Covenant on Economic, Social, and
Cultural Rights (1976)**
- Right to work
- Right to social security
- Right to protection of family
- Right to an adequate standard of living
- Right to education
- Right to health
- Right to join trade unions

## INSTRUMENTS PROVIDING PARTICULAR PROTECTION

International Convention on the Elimination of All Forms of Racial
Discrimination (1965)

Convention on the Elimination of All Forms of Discrimination Against Women
(1979)

Convention Against Torture and other Cruel, Inhuman and Degrading
Treatment or Punishment (1987)

Convention on the Rights of the Child (1989)

International Convention on the Protection of the Rights of All Migrant
Workers and Members of Their Families (1990)

## RULES REGARDING DETENTION AND TREATMENT OF OFFENDERS

Standard Minimum Rules for the Treatment of Prisoners (1955)

Principles of Medical Ethics (1982)

Standard Minimum Rules for the Administration of Juvenile Justice (1985)

## OTHER HUMAN RIGHTS INSTRUMENTS

Declaration on the Right to Development (1986)

Declaration on the Elimination of All Forms of Religious Intolerance
(1981)

Declaration on the Protection of Women and Children in Armed Conflicts
(1974)

Declaration on the Rights of Mentally Retarded Persons (1971)

---

*These instruments are described in more detail in United Nations (1992).

# Diverse Social Justice Perspectives: The Role of Critical Analysis

The diverse conceptualizations of social justice represent different popular perspectives about what social justice is or should be. So, when we say that social workers need to see social problems and individual troubles through a social justice lens, we are saying that it is important to recognize the various social justice lenses and the underlying value assumptions that support divergent views of what is just. Now that you have some familiarity with social justice concepts, we suggest you take a moment to do the following exercise.

Classroom Exercise 1.3  Discussion of Demands

The following scenario was described in Classroom Exercise 1.1, along with questions to help you examine your own social justice perspective. Read the scenario again and, in small groups, confer and come to some conclusions about the discussion question. This could also serve as a written assignment.

> Recently the workers at a major university went on strike to call attention to their demands. One of the demands was that all staff who have salaries up to $60,000 should get an across-the-board salary increase of $400 per month.

Discussion Question:
Assign each small group to take the position of one of the five perspectives on social justice: utilitarian, libertarian, egalitarian, the racial contract, and human rights. The group will then discuss how its assigned perspective might evaluate the workers' demands in regard to whether they are just and what changes might be made in the demand to make it just, according to your group's assigned theory. Each group will report its conclusions to the whole class. Be sure your conclusions are supported by the principles of the distributive justice theory assigned to your group.

# Differing Perspectives and Culturally Competent Social Work Practice

While there are differences within the profession regarding the definition of social justice, it is often proposed that the egalitarian theory is closest to traditional social work values and ethics. Wakefield (1988), for example, argues that "social work strives to ensure that no person is deprived of a fair minimum level of those basic social goods to which everyone is entitled," and supports Rawls's inclusion of self-respect in the list of social goods (p. 187). Yet, there is also evidence that, while perhaps holding to egalitarian principles as the ideal, social workers may tend to operate from a utilitarian perspective in practice (Conrad, 1988; Reisch & Taylor, 1983). For instance, terms such as *cost-benefit analysis* and *triage* strategies related to managed care realities might point to a utilitarian approach to promoting justice.

The first three contemporary theories (i.e., egalitarian, utilitarian, libertarian) are normative (i.e., what *should* be) and provide a useful tool for thinking about what social justice should be. However, they have serious limitations in that they do not explain why certain groups of people consistently get less justice. They also do not acknowledge, tackle, or explain the phenomenon of oppression. The racial contract, on the other hand, is a conceptual bridge between the normative (i.e., what *should* be) and the reality of race relations (i.e., racism and injustice). The human rights perspective can be seen as building on the racial contract's description of what *is* by proposing a universal meeting of the human needs of all as a solution. On the one hand, there is the world of mainstream philosophy (such as the three contemporary theories of distributive justice), which focuses discussions about justice and rights in the abstract. On the other hand, there is the worldview grounded in analysis of issues regarding domination, conquest, imperialism, colonialism, racism, slavery, apartheid, and reparations, which attends to the overwhelming presence of these events in the histories of many peoples.

The racial contract as a concept provides a conceptual tool for integrating issues of cultural diversity, social and economic justice, and the impact of oppression on populations at risk. To endorse and implement an *ideal social contract*, the *nonideal* contract as it exists needs to be demystified and discarded. A major goal of critical analysis is to identify and acknowledge the reality of oppression. Critical analysis of the way things *are* engages us in normative work, such as advocacy, to create movement toward a just world. Critical analysis facilitates our understanding of the social contract's history and how its values and concepts have functioned to rationalize oppression. In identifying underlying value assumptions of ideas, critical thinking illuminates the systematic and ubiquitous exclusion of oppression in traditional perspectives of social justice. Consider the issue of promoting social and economic justice in the following classroom exercise.

Classroom Exercise 1.4   Resource Limitations

Read the case example and discuss the questions that follow.
    Mary is a social worker who provides a range of comprehensive services to clients in a public welfare agency that has limited and increasingly shrinking resources. Her caseload consists of 50 individuals and families, most of whom are Native American people who live on a nearby reservation. One of Mary's clients is a single mother of three small children. Her refrigerator has been malfunctioning, so milk and other dairy product spoil within a few days. When Mary advocates for a new refrigerator, her supervisor denies the request on the basis of the fact that there are several families on the reservation who don't have a refrigerator at all, and the agency's severely limited resources should be used to obtain refrigerators for them first.
    Discuss the following questions regarding this situation:

1. Do you think the supervisor's decision in this case is just (fair) or unjust (unfair)?
2. What principles does the supervisor seem to be using as a basis for the decision? Which particular social justice perspective/theory is reflected?
3. What other decisions might be made in this situation? What

principles and social justice perspectives underlie those alternative decisions?

4. Discuss what a decision would look like if it were based on the racial contract and human rights perspectives.

# Conclusion: Identifying, Analyzing, and Responding to Social Injustices

In this chapter, we presented five contemporary perspectives to help you engage in critical thinking about your own beliefs about social justice and to challenge you to examine them through the lens of promoting social and economic justice for diverse populations. Distributive justice theory provides a basis for understanding the complexity of our notions about what social justice *should be* and the reality of social injustice as it currently exists. The racial contract is most consistent with this book's premise that diversity and social justice are inextricably entwined. Analysis of one's notions about social justice leads to a recognition that the beliefs one holds about social justice are race- and gender-based. This process highlights the presence of oppression, its dynamics, and how it shows up differentially in regard to diverse populations.

The racial contract reveals that some people are seen as expendable or undeserving and are thus excluded from the realm of social justice. That is to say, some people have not been included in or benefited from the social contract. They are vulnerable to the negative labeling placed on those groups with which they identify. Their oppression and exclusion are premised on stereotypes and prejudicial attitudes related to ethnocentrism. A human rights perspective of social justice provides the solution that all people are entitled to the same universal rights, without discrimination.

Social workers work with clients on a variety of levels—micro, meso, and macro. Concerns about human rights, social inequities, oppression, and other forms of injustice need to be identified on all levels. This chapter ends with a suggested assignment to help you take the next step of applying your skills in self-awareness, knowledge, and critical thinking and to advocate for social justice in an agency situation.

## Assignment 1.1  Analysis of an Agency Policy

The learning objective of this assignment is to help you examine an agency policy from a social justice perspective and develop strategies for promoting a more just policy.

Choose an agency policy from your field placement or agency of employment with which you have some concerns and analyze the policy and its impact on people from a social justice perspective. You may provide your analysis in a paper or as a presentation to the class. The analysis should include ways in which the policy perpetuates oppression of clients or staff. You should defend your position and discuss the pros and cons of alternative positions about the policy. Strategy steps for advocating change should be included in the analysis. The following questions are suggested as guides:

1. Describe the policy in detail.

2. Discuss how the policy negatively affects clients or staff; be specific about which people are being harmed and how.

3. Discuss who is benefiting from the policy; be specific.

4. On what basis do you determine that the policy is unjust? Make your case specifically and clearly.

5. Which of the five social justice perspectives presented in this chapter are you using to make your case that the policy is unjust?

6. What are alternative and differing views about the policy? Be sure to discuss fully the view about the policy that is different from yours.

7. Which of the five social justice perspectives presented in this chapter does this opposing view use to make its case?

8. What strategy steps do you propose for advocating for change? Be specific and realistic.

# References

Barker, R. L. (2003). *The social work dictionary* (5th ed.). Washington, DC: NASW Press.

Beverly, D. P., & McSweeney, E. A. (1987). *Social welfare and social justice.* Englewood Cliffs, NJ: Prentice-Hall.

Conrad, A. P. (1988). The role of field instructors in the transmission of social justice values. *Journal of Teaching in Social Work, 2*(2), 63–82.

Council on Social Work Education. (2001). *Educational policy and accreditation standards.* Alexandria, VA: Author.

Flynn, J. P. (1995). Social justice in social agencies. In R. L. Edwards (Ed.-in-Chief), *Encyclopedia of social work* (19th ed.) (pp. 2173–2179). Washington, DC: NASW Press.

Gil, D. (1998). *Confronting injustice and oppression: Concepts and strategies for social workers.* New York: Columbia University Press.

Hare, R. M. (1992). Justice and equality. In S. P. Sterba (Ed.), *Justice: Alternative political perspectives* (pp. 185–199). Belmont, CA: Wadsworth.

*Encyclopedia of social work* (19th ed.) (pp. 2173–2179). Washington, DC: NASW Press.

International Federation of Social Workers. (1994). *International declaration of ethical principles of social work.* Oslo, Norway: Author.

Mills, C. W. (1997). *The racial contract.* Ithaca, NY: Cornell.

National Association of Social Workers. (1996). *Code of Ethics.* Washington, DC: Author.

Nozick, R. (1974). *Anarchy, state, and utopia.* New York: Basic Books.

Nussbaum, M. (2000). *Women and human development: The capabilities approach.* Cambridge, UK: Cambridge University Press.

Nussbaum, M. (2001). *Upheavals of thought: The intelligence of emotions.* Cambridge, UK: Cambridge University Press.

Rawls, J. (1971). *A theory of justice.* Cambridge, MA: Harvard University Press.

Reisch, M. (2002). Defining social justice in a socially unjust world. *Families in Society, 83*(4), 343–354.

Reisch, M., & Taylor, C. T. (1983). Ethical guidelines for cutback management: A preliminary approach. *Administration in Social Work, 7*(3/4), 59–72.

Sidgwick, H. (1966). *The methods of ethics.* New York: Dover.

Sterba, J.P. (1985). From liberty to welfare. *Social Theory and Practice, 11*(3), 285-305.

United Nations. (1992). *Teaching and learning about human rights: A manual for schools of social work and the social work profession.* New York: Author.

Van Soest, D. (2003). Advancing social and economic justice. In D. Lum, *Culturally competent practice: A framework for understanding diverse groups and justice issues* (pp. 350–351). Pacific Grove, CA: Brooks/Cole.

van Wormer, K. (2004). *Confronting oppression, restoring justice: From policy analysis to social action.* Alexandria, VA: Council on Social Work Education.

Wakefield, J. C. (1988, June). Psychotherapy, distributive justice, and social work. Part I: Distributive justice as a conceptual framework for social work. *Social Service Review,* 187–210.

Young, I. M. (1990). *Justice and the politics of difference.* Princeton, NJ: Princeton University Press.

Zinn, H. (1997). *The Zinn Reader: Writings on disobedience and democracy.* New York: Seven Stories Press.

# Chapter Two
# A Framework for Culturally Competent Social Work Practice: Uniting Cultural Diversity and Social Justice

A primary premise of this book is that culturally competent social work involves effective interventions with diverse clients coupled with a commitment to promote social justice. This means that two of social work's professional responsibilities are inextricably linked: 1) to provide culturally competent services, and 2) to promote social and economic justice. Linking these two responsibilities means that it is important to understand the patterns, dynamics, and consequences of oppression as they affect historically disadvantaged groups in relation to all diversities, including ethnicity, race,[1] gender, sexual orientation, disability, the elderly, and other vulnerable groups. This perspective is based on the significance of the intersection between socioeconomic status and diversity. The impact and experience of one cannot be comprehended without understanding it in the context of the other. Each factor speaks to the presence of privilege, entitlement, and or/constraint in the lives of individuals and families.

But understanding oppression is not enough. Social workers need knowledge and skills to promote social and economic justice effectively (Council on Social Work Education, 1992, 2001). In an increasingly diverse and inequitable society, social workers now more than ever face the double

---

1. We use ethnicity, people of color, and race interchangeably in reference to what have been called ethnic minorities. All of these refer to values, beliefs, heritage, and life experience that influence the formation of social identity. In that all groups have national origin heritage, this term is applied to all groups in relation to their social and racial identity. The term race is used with the understanding that it is a social construct and has no biological evidence.

challenges of understanding societal oppression *and* translating that understanding into actions designed to facilitate social change for social justice. The challenges are daunting.

This chapter provides a context and theoretical foundation for learning processes aimed at helping you meet the challenges successfully. It begins with an examination of some persistent issues and obstacles inherent in learning about cultural diversity for social justice and then presents a conceptual framework that unites cultural diversity issues and social justice. Before reading further, we suggest you do the following reflection exercise to explore your personal experiences, values, beliefs, and feelings. Chapter 3 discusses cultural competency in detail, including definition and relevant issues, dynamics, and practice implications.

**REFLECTION EXERCISE 2.1 CULTURAL DIVERSITY FOR SOCIAL JUSTICE**

1. Take a moment to consider the words *cultural diversity*. Write down all the thoughts and feelings those words evoke. Just brainstorm without censoring yourself, knowing that no one else will see what you wrote.

2. Take a moment to consider the words *social justice*. Write down all the thoughts and feelings those words evoke.

3. Put the two terms together—*cultural diversity for social justice*. Again, write down any thoughts and feelings you have.

4. Now look at your three lists of thoughts and feelings and consider the possibility of sharing what you wrote with others in the class. What would you be comfortable sharing? What would you be uncomfortable sharing?

5. What are the two or three things that would make it difficult for you to talk about diversity and social justice issues?

# Why Is Learning About Cultural Diversity and Social Justice So Difficult?

People often respond with resistance, distress, and anger when faced with cultural diversity and social justice issues. Expressions such as the following illustrate such experiences of discomfort: "Why do we have to talk about race all the time? We all have problems in life!" "We have made great progress in this country—why do we focus on the negative and difference so much?" "Why aren't we focusing on how we are all human?" "This is the best country in the world in terms of equal rights and freedom" "I am tired of being blamed for injustice!" What is behind such statements of resistance? While there are many issues and obstacles on the journey to cultural competence, three are particularly significant. First, feelings of fear and anger can make it difficult to listen and talk about issues related to access to social power that is based on difference. Second, there is no coherent framework that speaks to basic human experiences and that is truly inclusive of diversity and social justice, making it difficult to conceptualize and, therefore, fully understand the issues and dynamics. Finally, difficulties are posed by current social and political realities such as increased backlash and absence of collective social action for social change.

Each of these three obstacles is discussed in more depth below.

## Exposing Our Dirty Secrets and Confronting Our Fear and Anger

Much of the fear and anger that comes up for White ethnics around discussions related to cultural diversity may be rooted in the secret of White privilege. The first obstacle to learning about cultural diversity for social justice is related to this secret. Bob Jensen (1998), a journalism professor, described what White privilege sounds like in an editorial, entitled "Wake Up to White Privilege":

> I am sitting in my University of Texas office, talking to a very bright and very conservative white student about affirmative action in college admissions, which he opposes and I support.

The student says he wants a level playing field with no unearned advantages for anyone. I ask him whether he thinks that in the United States being white has advantages. Have either of us, I ask, ever benefited from being white in a world run mostly by white people? Yes, he concedes, there is something real and tangible we could call white privilege.

So, if we live in a world of white privilege—unearned white privilege—how does that affect your notion of a level playing field? I ask. He paused for a moment and said, "That really doesn't matter."

That statement, I suggested to him, reveals the ultimate white privilege: The privilege to acknowledge you have unearned privilege but ignore what it means (handout).

Further, in the editorial, Jensen wrote, "the dirty secret that we white people carry with us in this world of white privilege is that some of what we have is unmerited" (Jensen, 1998). This secret suggested by Jensen illuminates the context in which this book approaches cultural diversity and education for multicultural competence in social work. The secret, of pretending that people benefit based on what they deserve through merit, significantly hinders direct and honest dialogue about White supremacy and White privilege.

## REFLECTION EXERCISE 2.2
## UNPACKING/PACKING OUR PRIVILEGES: PART 1*

Imagine that you have a backpack filled with special circumstances and conditions that you experience that you did not earn but that you have been made to feel are yours by birth, by citizenship, and by virtue of being a conscientious, law-abiding, "normal" person of goodwill. If you are White, imagine that these privileges have been given to you because of your skin color. If you are a person of color, imagine that the privileges are not in your backpack, but that you would have them if you were White. If you are White, imagine, as you list the privileges you have, that you are taking them out of your backpack (unpacking your privileges) so you can look at them. If you are a person of color, imagine, as you list the privileges you would have if you were White, that you are putting them into your backpack as if they were yours. List at least six privileges.

Now look at your list and reflect on how it feels to consider unpacking your privileges or putting privileges heretofore denied into your pack. Consider having a straightforward discussion in class about White privilege. What excites you about such a discussion? What fears might you have?

---

*Reflection exercises 2.2, 2.3, and 2.4 are based on the work of Peggy McIntosh (1995).

In his editorial, Jensen addresses some of the fears that keep people from talking directly about diversity when he describes his personal fear of not being special, his fear of not being worthy of his successes, his fear that what he always thought he had earned through his own effort may, in reality, be more a function of being born White rather than a result of brains and hard work. For those who benefit from White privilege, this kind of fear and anger may pose one of the biggest obstacles to learning about diversity and social justice.

Ideas and discussions that relate to race and difference evoke particularly primitive feelings in all people, because, after all, people like to see themselves as well-meaning individuals. The realization that they are part of the problem of racism, and that they simultaneously benefit from it, often elicits fervent responses in White social workers, regardless of their status as students, faculty, or practitioners. This is often complicated by the presence of deep-seated feelings  of which they may be unaware of on a conscious level. Often, there is genuine shock at allegations of collusion with a system of dominance, particularly when racism is linked to extremists, such as in hate crimes, or with institutional practices, such as redlining in banks. People have a sense of dread and terror that at any moment they might err with respect to racism by revealing something offensive, suggesting that they don't know the rules and, therefore, don't know how to prevent an insensitive comment from escaping their lips. White people may feel confused because they may not know what it means for people of color to navigate through hostile, unwelcoming terrain. They don't know what it means to have to deal with unresponsive institutions whose cooperation is needed for one to achieve basic essentials (e.g., employment, housing, equitable salary, health services). After all, the terrain through which most White folks have navigated has functioned in their best interests.

The opposite has been the reality for most people of color. In an article, titled "Whites in Multicultural Education: Rethinking Our Role," Gary Howard writes: "Throughout most of our history, there has been no reason why White Americans, for their own survival or success, have needed to be sensitive to the cultural perspectives of other groups. This is not a luxury available to people of color, [whose] daily survival depends on knowledge of White America. . . . To be successful in mainstream institutions, people of color in the U.S. need to be bicultural—able to play by the rules of their own cultural community and able to play the game according to the rules established by the dominant culture. For most White Americans, on the other hand, there is only one game, and they have traditionally been on the winning team" (1993, p. 38).

Talking about race is difficult because of the tremendous gulf of experience and meaning between individuals who are positioned differently based on their access to sociopolitical power and privilege. So people tend to not talk about it. Or they don't want to talk about it. Or they talk about it in safe terms, always mindful not to talk about the secret of White privilege. Or they talk about it exclusively in psychological terms, choosing to focus on behavioral factors (e.g., feelings, thoughts, interpersonal communication) and thus avoiding the institutional nature of the problem. In social work practice we often use the expression, "People are only as sick as their secrets." While racism is clearly more than a "disease," not talking directly and honestly about White privilege allows White people to keep the truth from themselves, which means they don't have to change. It is this resistance to the truth that makes it very difficult for White people to listen to people of color. This resistance places responsibility on the person of color to be the one to initiate and stimulate discussion on racism issues to enlighten others. The following exercise is intended to stimulate classroom discussion about how people experience talking about race. Note that in the exercise and throughout the book, the terms *race* and *people of color* are used interchangeably.

---

Classroom Exercise 2.1
Let's Talk About Talking About Race

If you are a person of color, write down as many endings to this sentence stem as you can spontaneously write in 3 minutes: "As a person of color, I . . . ." Try to not censor yourself in any way.

If you are a White person, write down as many endings to this sentence stem as you can spontaneously write in 3 minutes. "As a White person, I . . ." Try not to censor yourself in any way.

Now choose three or four of the sentences that you would feel comfortable sharing with others in the class. Choose the one or two sentences that you would feel most uncomfortable sharing. Discuss your thoughts with one other person in class in a dyad or with a small group.

Once everyone has shared, talk about how it felt to focus a discussion on race.

---

## THE SECRET OF MALE PRIVILEGE

The secret about a system of advantage for Whites isn't the only secret that blocks us in our attempts to address issues of diversity for social justice. Gender in the United States consists of unearned advantage and dominance for males. Again, the secret related to gender is that some of what males have is unmerited. Fear and anger rooted in this secret make it difficult for males to take what females say seriously, particularly in relation to male privilege, in the same way that White privilege makes it difficult for White people to listen to people of color. In her essay, "White Privilege and Male Privilege," Peggy McIntosh (1995) describes how the system of gender privilege, like racial privilege, becomes invisible to the males who benefit from it, even though it colors the everyday life of both males and females.

**REFLECTION EXERCISE 2.3**
**UNPACKING/PACKING OUR PRIVILEGES: PART 2**

Imagine that you have a backpack filled with special circumstances and conditions that you experience that you did not earn but that you have been made to feel are yours by birth, by citizenship, and by virtue of being a conscientious, law-abiding, "normal" person of goodwill. If you are a male, imagine that these privileges have been given to you because of your gender. If you are a female, imagine the privileges that are not in your backpack but that you would have if you were male. If you are male, imagine, as you list the privileges you have, that you are taking them out of your backpack (unpacking your privileges) so you can look at them. If you are a female, imagine, as you list the privileges you would have if you were male, that you are putting them into your backpack as if they were yours. List at least six privileges.

Now look at your list and reflect on how it feels to consider unpacking your privileges or putting privileges heretofore denied into your pack. Consider having a straightforward, open discussion in class about male privilege. What excites you about such a discussion? What concerns and fears might you have?

## THE SECRET OF HETEROSEXUAL PRIVILEGE

McIntosh (1995) further points out that race and gender are not the only advantaging systems at work. The secret is that some of what people in other categories possess is also unmerited. Unearned privileges are granted by a system that advantages some people due to their sexual orientation, socioeconomic class, age, ability (mental and physical), nationality, or religion. In relation to heterosexual privilege, McIntosh asserts that "this is still a [bigger] taboo subject than race privilege: the daily ways in which heterosexual privilege endows some persons with comfort or power, provides supports, assets, approvals, and rewards those who live or expect to live in heterosexual pairs. Unpacking and owning those privileges is still more difficult, owing to the deep imbeddedness of heterosexual advantage and dominance and stricter taboos surrounding these" (p. 85).

The first obstacle to learning about diversity for social justice is the fear and anger rooted in these secrets of unmerited privilege that keep people from talking honestly and directly about systems of advantage. Delving into feelings about privilege is like roaming into an area rife with emotional land mines, yet the understanding and insight that develop are worth the effort.

## REFLECTION EXERCISE 2.4
## UNPACKING/PACKING OUR PRIVILEGES: PART 3

Imagine that you have a backpack filled with special circumstances and conditions that you experience that you did not earn but that you have been made to feel are yours by birth, by citizenship, and by virtue of being a conscientious, law-abiding, "normal" person of goodwill. If your sexual orientation is heterosexuality, imagine that these privileges have been given to you because you are hetero-sexual. If you are a gay, lesbian, bisexual, or transgender person, imagine the privileges that are not in your backpack but that you would have if you were heterosexual. If you are a heterosexual person, imagine, as you list the privileges you have, that you are taking them out of your backpack (unpacking your privileges) so you can look at them. If you are a gay, lesbian, bisexual, or transgender person imagine, as you list the privileges you would have if you were heterosexual, that you are putting them into your backpack as if they were yours. List at least six privileges.

Now look at your list and reflect on how it feels to consider unpacking your privileges or putting privileges heretofore denied into your pack. Consider having a straightforward discussion in class about heterosexual privilege. What excites you about such a discussion? What concerns and fears might you have?

# Creating a Coherent Conceptual Framework That Speaks to Human Experience

A second obstacle to developing cultural competence is that the social work profession lacks a coherent conceptual framework to address diversity and social justice issues that can be applied to a wide range of professional knowledge areas, such as conducting assessments, engaging with individuals and families, theories of human behavior, policy formulation, implementation and analysis, working with communities, and conducting research. All too often theoretical approaches ignore or deny the presence of privilege and oppression that underlie the secrets presented above. When significant factors such as power and privilege are disregarded, professional practice can be compromised in that valuable information regarding critical aspects of the client's life experiences is lost.

Culturally competent practice within a social justice perspective is premised on a willingness to look at the dominant side of the oppression equation rather than opting for a "watered down" version of the experiences of people who have been historically disadvantaged that dismisses their historical context and social power position. As will be apparent later in this chapter, this book maintains that understanding race and racism is basic to comprehending how oppression is played out in relation to other target groups and, thus, a first step in developing cultural competence becomes a willingness to look at the White side of the racist equation. Edwards-Orr (1988) warns against attempts to develop sensitivity toward socially and politically marginalized people without exploring the factors associated with their exclusion. When such factors are ignored, those in a privileged position essentially place responsibility on those in a target or subordinate position to describe the experience of oppression and its effects in their lives. This thinking feeds into using language such as "the Black problem," an example of blaming the victim, and ignores factors related to social power. This thinking also diverts the focus away from privilege and the examination of values, beliefs, and practices related to privilege. An approach that focuses on the "other," who is different, reinforces the myths that cultural diversity is about the "other" and that it is an entitlement program for groups such as African Americans, Latinos, Asians, Native Americans, women, poor people, and gay/lesbian/bisexual/transgender people. The perception underlying these myths is that these groups are receiving undeserved benefits.

It is important to ask: "Why are some groups marginalized?" "Who benefits from their marginalization?" When these questions are ignored, the essential task of integrating cultural diversity matters with issues of social justice is neglected. When these questions are explored, they lead to further questions, such as: How do systems of oppression shape the life experiences of both those who are disadvantaged *and* those who are advantaged by them? Thinking about the transformation of "unjust and oppressive social, economic, and political institutions into just and nonoppressive alternatives" (Gil, 1998, p. 1) requires the vigorous effort of exposing the secret of privilege, thus bringing us full circle.

## Current Social and Political Realities

The third issue and obstacle to addressing diversity for social justice issues is current social and political realities. The sociopolitical environment is in constant flux, with changing regional, national, and global events. In the current climate of a deeply troubled and increasingly polarized nation and world, it is important not to underestimate the difficulty of engaging in the kind of learning necessary for culturally competent practice, given the reality of present-day structural and institutional leadership and practices. Critical thinking about the values and beliefs that support diversity for social justice is not widely supported. Social work—as a product of its society—reflects the power structure of U.S. societal control by a privileged class based on ethnicity and socioeconomic class. When it comes to discrimination and oppressive systems, social work has historically been more successful in responding to social injustice than it has been at integrating this goal into its professional agenda. This has been especially true in relation to race.

Critical examination of the contemporary role of power and privilege in both society and the social work profession is more difficult due to the current climate of antiaffirmative action and antimulticulturalism. The myth that multicultural education and the growth of diversity groups will divide our country and undermine its unity seems to be gaining in popularity, as illustrated by Arthur Schlesinger's 1991 book, *The Disuniting of America:*

*Reflections on a Multicultural Society*, and Samuel Huntington's book, *Who Are We? The Challenges to American's National Identity*. This myth falsely assumes that our nation is already united and that meritocracy exists. It ignores the reality that our country is, and always has been, deeply divided along lines of race, gender, class, sexual orientation, and other groupings. Yet the myth persists and is an obstacle to our attempts to develop an approach to social work practice that unites diversity and social justice.

The three obstacles discussed in this section—issues of privilege, lack of a coherent conceptual framework that unites diversity and social justice, and current social and political realities—create substantial barriers to the development of cultural competence within a social justice framework. In the following section we address these obstacles by providing three essential components of a conceptual framework that are aimed at helping to overcome the barriers.

# A Conceptual Framework That Unites Cultural Diversity and Social Justice

This section begins with a parable using a river metaphor (Derman-Sparks & Brunson Phillips, 1997) that captures some of the concerns related to the task of integrating cultural competency and social justice.

> Once upon a time a woman, strolling along a riverbank, hears a cry for help and, seeing a drowning person, rescues him. She no sooner finishes administering artificial respiration when another cry requires another rescue. Again, she has only just helped the second person when a third call for help is heard. After a number of rescues, she begins to realize that she is pulling some people out of the river more than once. By this time the rescuer is exhausted and resentful, feeling that if people are stupid or careless enough to keep landing in the river, they can rescue themselves. She is too annoyed, tired, and frustrated to look around her.
>
> Shortly after, another woman walking along the river hears the cries for help and begins rescuing people. She, however, wonders why so many people are drowning in this river. Looking around her, she sees a hill where

something seems to be pushing people off. Realizing this as the source of the drowning problem, she is faced with a difficult dilemma: If she rushes uphill, people presently in the river will drown; if she stays at the river pulling them out, more people will be pushed in. What can she do? (pp. 1–2)

The second woman's thoughts suggest that she may be questioning why these people share particular characteristics and if a selection process is under way. If racism, sexism, heterosexism, classism, ageism, and other forms of oppression are defined as the force on the hill, then this metaphor suggests three alternative solutions for social workers: 1) rescue people in trouble and return them to the oppressive conditions that caused the problem; 2) after rescuing people, teach them how to manage their problems so that if they "get pushed into the river again" at least they won't drown; and 3) organize with people to destroy the source of the problem.

The educational framework proposed in this book opts for the third position. Social workers need to do more than respond to the symptoms or consequences of oppressive conditions; they need to develop strategies for responding to the source of oppression. Most important, they need to reevaluate their own role, on a personal and professional level, in the continuation of oppression. Social work practice ultimately must be about recognizing the source of the problem and then understanding how to eliminate the problem on the hill.

## REFLECTION EXERCISE 2.5  PARABLE

Below is a list of questions for you to answer in reaction to the parable. We suggest that you write down your responses first and then discuss them with a group of your peers.

- If the river represents a situation of oppression or disadvantage, what is it like to be in the river?

- In other words, what are the conditions and processes of oppression and how do they affect people's lives and life chances?

•Who are the people being pushed into the river? What characteristics do they have in common? What is the singular facet of their experience that puts them at risk?

•Which people are *not* being pushed into the river? What are their common characteristics? How do they benefit from having others pushed into the river?

•If the force on the hill that is pushing people into the river represents racism, sexism, classism, heterosexism, and other systems of advantage, how does the force operate? How much of this is to be understood in individual, psychological terms and how much as a "business as usual" patterning of institutional practices, a mix of this and other factors?

•What happens so that people who used to be in the river and got out then go up the hill to push people who look like them in the river?

•What role can social workers learn to take in helping the people who are pushed into the river?

•What organizational, collaborative, and advocacy skills can social workers develop to eliminate the force that is pushing people into the river?

Critical examination of the river metaphor identifies the relevant issues that need to be addressed conceptually. Four fundamental components of a coherent conceptual framework for cultural competency within a social justice approach are proposed here. These are: 1) acknowledgment of the centrality of the social construction of race and the practice of racism in understanding all oppressions (i.e., the "isms"); 2) recognition of racism as "a mode of human relations involving domination and exploitation" that produces a socioeconomic class system (Gil, 1998, p. 10); 3) appreciation of the complex interaction of racism with the systemic dynamics of oppressions based on gender, class, sexual orientation, ability, age, and the concept of multiple identities; and 4) attention to the learning process even when engaged in it. We discuss each of the four components below.

# The Centrality of Race and Racism

The first component identifies race and racism as a foundation for understanding other forms of oppression, such as sexism, classism, heterosexism, ageism, and oppression based on ability, and so on. In this way, understanding race and racism is seen as the basis for understanding cultural competence. Race always has and continues to have a central role in our country, and understanding White privilege—and a corresponding investment in Whiteness—is essential to eradicating racism. As Lipsitz (1998), eloquently notes: "Although reproduced in new form in every era, the possessive investment in whiteness has always been influenced by its origins in the racialized history of the United States—by its legacy of slavery and segregation, of 'Indian' extermination and immigrant restriction, of conquest and colonialism" (p. 3). In his book, *Two Nations: Black and White, Separate, Hostile, Unequal*, political science professor Andrew Hacker (1992) provides overwhelming evidence of exactly how completely racial issues shape the thinking of everyone in the United States. More than any other oppression, racism has been used historically to assign status and power based on racial indicators, such as skin color. Of all the forms of exclusion, discrimination, and power-assignment that exist in this country—and there are many— "none is so deeply rooted, persistent, and intractable as that based on color" (Hopps, 1982, p. 3). While the dynamics of all forms of oppression are not fully informed by racism, understanding how racism is maintained is central to comprehending the dynamics of oppression and how oppression plays out in relation to other target groups because of what can be learned from the important parallels and intersections between racism and other forms of oppression and the intractability of oppression based on race

## THE CONCEPT OF RACE: A SOCIAL CONSTRUCT

Many think of race as an inherent, innate quality that underlies significant differences in the human race. Race is, in fact, a socially constructed category linked to relations of power and processes of social and political struggle. As a social construct, it is a relational and political concept. It is a construct whose meaning changes over time, by legal statute, and is subject to personal definition. Even though it is socially constructed, "race," like gender and sexual orientation, is "real" in the sense that it has actual, though changing, effects on how people see themselves, on interactions between and among individuals, and on interactions between individuals and institutions. It has tangible and complex effects on peoples' sense of self, experiences, and life opportunities. For example, whether one thinks in terms of seeking a "job" or developing a "career" is based on what a person believes he or she can hope for and plan on. Limitations imposed by societal stereotyping pose obstacles and limit enthusiasm for pursuing long-term goals. Culturally competent practice addresses such obstacles by focusing on the role of social and political factors in understanding peoples lives, rather than engaging in reductionist simplistic thinking about unfounded innate qualities. With such a focus, choices people make can be examined in an unbiased fashion within the context of environmental obstacles.

Recognition of powerful environmental constraints does not suggest that people's choices be dismissed. Rather, strengths-based, empowerment-focused professional actions require recognition of individual choice within the context of resources and access. Culturally competent interactions within a social justice approach are based on an understanding that individual choice is made within the context of the individual's social power and social, political realities. This is discussed further in chapter 3.

Many historical examples abound regarding the social construction of race and the subsequent categorization of social groups in our country. For example, Japanese Americans, who were once considered "non-White" and "Oriental,"[2] are now identified in the broad category of "Asian and Pacific Islander" (Omi & Winant, 1986). At the time of their arrival, Jewish people were kept at the margin of dominant society, because they were not Christians; Catholics were not regarded as "White," and Italian Americans, Irish Americans, and Latinos, at different times, have been viewed as both "White" and "non-White" (Hacker, 1992).

Historically, it is clear that the question is not "Who *is* White?" It might be more appropriate to ask, "Who *may* be considered White?" since evidence

---

2. "Oriental" refers to the European colonialist perspective regarding the Easterner, that is, east of the center, meaning east of Europe.

suggests that arbitrary factors related to power and validation are implicated. In a sense, those who have already received the "White" designation can be seen as belonging to a club, from whose sanctum it is decided whether new members are needed or wanted as well as the proper pace of new admissions: The "White club" is, as much as anything else, one of privilege and power and its members have always had the power to expand its domain. While it has admitted people of all ethnicities over time, it has and continues to be particularly reluctant to absorb people of African descent (Hacker, 1992, p. 9).

Although race is a social construct with ambiguous meaning and is used to achieve political purposes, racism is real, and this country's racist legacy is one of conquests and genocide of its indigenous native peoples, colonialism, slavery, and segregation. Racism is different from prejudice, which is a personal, psychological phenomenon characterized by prejudgments and biased beliefs about individuals. Racism is also different from discrimination, which refers to action taken against others based on biased beliefs. Racism is set apart from the former two behaviors because it is an institutionalized system of advantage grounded in social, political, and economic power. Social arrangements of advantage, based on an ideology of White supremacy, deprive and diminish people of color while offering preference, support, and opportunity to those perceived as White (Knowles & Prewitt, 1969). This suggests at least a couple of implications. One is that "racist" behavior, by definition, is practiced by those whose social identity and privilege is supported and validated by dominant society. Second, prejudice is not necessary for individuals to carry out racist institutional practices, because the specific practices are part of systematic, program-based policies.

For White people, engaging in the struggle to comprehend racism often results in resistance to grasping its institutional nature. Racism is viewed as an issue that people of color face and with which they have to struggle (after all, they are the ones being pushed into the river in disproportionate numbers). Racism is not seen as an issue that involves or implicates White people. This view of racism has far-reaching consequences for how one approaches and thinks about antiracism work. Due to the difficulty of grasping the institutional nature of racism, White people often view antiracism work as an act of compassion for an "other" (i.e., they can pull the "others" out of the river). It also may be seen as an optional extra project, perhaps even an important social work commitment, but not one intimately and organically linked to White people's own lives. In short, racism can be conceived as something external to White people, rather than as a system that shapes the daily experiences and sense of self of *all* of us. Truly understanding the institutional nature of racism means noticing that racism distorts everyone's sense of self, regardless of ethnic or racial background. The difference is that Whites, who enjoy White privilege, distort in the direction of overestimation of self, and people of color distort in the direction of underestimation of self.

## WHITENESS

The process of learning about cultural diversity for social justice must include people with privilege, in this case White people. A beginning question is: How do race and racism shape White people's lives? In her book, *The Social Construction of Whiteness: White Women, Race Matters* (1993), Frankenberg writes: "In the same way that both men's and women's lives are shaped by their gender and that both heterosexual and lesbian women's experiences in the world are marked by their sexuality, both white people and people of color live racially structured lives. In other words, any system of differentiation shapes those on whom it bestows privilege as well as those it oppresses. . . . [thus] in a social context where white people have too often viewed themselves as nonracial or racially neutral, it is crucial to look at the 'racialness' of white experience" (p. 1). Thus, this book proposes that learning about diversity for social justice must include exploration of the question: How does "Whiteness" shape people's lives?

Frankenberg suggests that using the name *Whiteness* shifts it from the unnamed status that is a consequence of dominance and is taken as "normal." Institutional racism is hidden behind the daily practices of hard-working, well-meaning White people. Institutional racism typically isn't ugly. Rather than being expressed through hostile, racial slurs, it is often wrapped in righteous proclamations of tradition, fairness, and high standards. Rather than being a rare incident, it is woven into the fabric of our historically racist society. Subtle and slippery forms of institutional racism are silently and invisibly tearing at the fiber of our schools and our society. And "Whiteness" is at its core.

To look at "Whiteness," then, is to look head-on at a site of dominance. And, as Frankenberg points out, it is much more difficult for White people to say, "Whiteness has nothing to do with me—I'm not white" than it is to say, "Race has nothing to do with me—I'm not racist" (p. 6). To speak of "Whiteness" is to assign *everyone* a place in the dynamics of racism. This emphasizes that dealing with racism is not in actuality an *option* for White people. Rather, racism virtually shapes White people's lives and identities in a way that is inseparable from other facets of daily life. As Frankenberg argues, there *is* a cultural/racial specificity to White people, at times more obvious to people who are not White than to those who are.

There are a couple of key points to keep in mind here. First, while racism shapes the lives of all people, there is a gulf of difference in the experience of racism between White people and people of color. Second, at this time in U.S. history, Whiteness as an ethnic identity is often presented in terms of the "White pride" of the politically conservative far right. It should be noted that when North Americans of European descent celebrate being "White," this is quite different from ethnic White people affirming their cultural, national heritage. The former—celebrating Whiteness—represents, in the current political climate, a White supremacist act, an act of backlash. The latter represents a celebration of one's ethnic culture.

Within the context of antiracist work, the challenge is to make visible and undermine White culture's ties to domination, keeping perspective on the differential effects of socioeconomic class standing. Back to the parable of people drowning in the river, it means being able to see White people—even well-meaning White social workers—as part of the force that is pushing people in the river.

---

**REFLECTION EXERCISE 2.6    RACE-BASED EXPERIENCES GROWING UP***

1. When were you first aware of yourself as a member of a particular racial group?

2. When were you first aware of people from other races? What races?

REFLECTION EXERCISE 2.6    RACE-BASED EXPERIENCES GROWING UP
(continued)

3. When did you first witness or experience someone being treated differently because of his or her racial group?

4. When was a time that you were proud of your racial identity?

5. When was a time you realized that you would be treated differently because of your race?

6. What are some times when you had or have friends from different racial groups?

7. Have there been any other significant events in your life related to race or racism?

---

*From Wijeyesinghe, Griffin, & Love (1997, p. 90).

# The Powerful Role of Socioeconomic Class

The second component of this book's conceptual framework that unites cultural diversity and social justice points to the role of a person's socioeconomic class in inferring privilege. This component views class privilege as parallel to White privilege. People of all races and ethnicities are victims of oppression based on class (i.e., are poor), and there is considerable class inequality among White people in the United States as well as between White people and people of color. Understanding racism, however, involves being cognizant of how oppression creates a class system based on skin color. Knowledge of the history of U.S. racism is essential to understand how its deep roots continue to nurture current forms of racism that result in race-specific socioeconomic inequity. In the United States, the colonization and devastation of a flourishing Native American civilization, the importation of Africans as slaves, the expropriation of land from Mexico in the Southwest, and the exploitation of Asian labor in building railroads and mining gold combined to lay the economic, political, and ideological foundation for the present structural relationships of racism (Howard, 1993).

To study the history of peoples of color in this country is to make clear the common elements of oppression. For example, exploitation of various ethnic groups for different purposes and at different points in history becomes evident. This recognition is potentially a basis for developing the bonds of solidarity that are necessary in advocacy efforts. When social power differences based on socioeconomic class position are factored into one's thinking about oppression based on color, it becomes evident that effects of class can mediate the effects of racism. Although it is unproductive to engage in comparative ranking about who is most oppressed, it is useful to consider, for example, the consequences of the oppression experienced by an upper-class, married African American female compared to a White, single, undereducated mother of three minor children.

When White people open themselves to learning about the historical perspectives and cultural experiences of people of color, much of what they discover is often seen as incompatible with their image of a democratic nation based on fairness. They may feel caught in a state of cognitive dissonance. They see that the success of the European venture in this country rests on acts of inhumanity. Yet, traditional education asserts that our European ancestors built a free and democratic land (Howard, 1993). Such cognitive dissonance is not easy to deal with in that it stirs up much feeling and a need to relieve the tension.

Being confronted with the harsh realities of history exposes the secret of White privilege, the creation of an economically privileged class, and the effects of class privilege. This may trigger feelings of hostility and fear in some. Well-intentioned people, who can understand and behave sensitively yet who harbor ambivalence, often feel guilt. People need to help each other to move beyond such negative responses and find a personally chosen place of authentic engagement with social change. A first step is to approach both the past and the present with a new sense of honesty. Facing the realities of history is the beginning of liberation. Both a dismal lack of historical perspective in the media and a strong emphasis on individual choice in the dominant culture diminish the value of viewing behavior in its historical context. It is important not to fall into a kind of disillusioned confession about the sins of one's ancestors. The healing response for those who have benefited from and those who have been disadvantaged by oppression is assuming responsibility and taking action (Howard, 1993, p. 40).

Thus far two components of this book's framework for culturally competent practice have been presented and the following points emphasized:

- It is important to develop a thorough understanding of racism as central to the formation, history, and current realities of U.S. society.

- Racism is viewed as an institutional not a psychological phenomenon.

- The construct of race shapes the identities, experiences, and potential class position of both people of color and White people.

- Social workers have a significant role to play in transforming racist systems and institutions into nonracist alternatives that promote social, political, and economic equity.

- Everyone is embedded in the problem of racism in the United States, and it needs to be dealt with collaboratively, jointly, and with shared accountability.

## The Complex Interaction of Multiple Social Identities

The third component of the conceptual framework highlights how racism interacts with the systemic dynamics of socioeconomic class and gender oppression. Understanding the dynamics of race and racism facilitates comprehension of the dynamics of oppression experienced by other groups. All people of color are targeted by racism. However, factors such as class, gender, sexual orientation, age, ability, and other social identities influence the ways in which racism may manifest itself in a particular person's life.

Correspondingly, all White people automatically have institutionalized White privilege. However, all White people do not reap its benefits equally. Class, gender, and sexual orientation, along with other aspects of identity, influence how much and in what ways individuals experience and benefit from their "Whiteness."

The intersection of the four identities of race, class, gender, and sexual orientation is the subject of considerable, sometimes heated, disagreement in many corners of personal and public life. Questions arise and arguments abound regarding which of these institutional forms of oppression came first or is the worst, a game of "competitive oppressions." This book maintains that race remains central to American life as an ongoing theme in U.S. history. The effects of racism are sufficiently powerful that potential bonds for joining in advocacy against social injustice and exploitation can be and often are undermined on the basis of race prejudice and discrimination. Thus, organizing efforts can be threatened and undermined by what may be false divisions. One must ask, what is going on that we don't often see coalitions of African Americans, Asians, Latinos, the elderly, those with disabilities, youth groups, and others? Thankfully, some of this is seen, particularly in urban settings, but hardly at all. Why not?

## COMMON IDEOLOGICAL UNDERPINNINGS OF FOUR OPPRESSIONS

Justifications for oppression based on gender, class, and sexual orientation are often similar to those that justify racism. While the denigration of an entire people on the basis of race is justified by an ideology of White supremacy and racial inferiority, likewise the depreciation of all females on the basis of gender is justified by an ideology of male superiority that insists that females are less intelligent and logical and more emotional and irrational. Similarly, disparagement of an entire people on the basis of sexual orientation is justified by insistence on mental and moral deficiencies. And the defamation of an entire people on the basis of economic status is justified by class superiority. For example, in the 19th century science was used to prove the biological inferiority of poor people and to propose a causal connection between poor people's lack of wealth and their lack of accomplishment and merit.

Diversity education for social justice requires an examination of the effects of the interlocking oppressions of racism, sexism, classism, and heterosexism on individual and group experiences related to power and privilege. Back to the parable presented earlier, it is important to understand that the force that pushes people into the river does so in a complicated yet systematic way. The overrepresentation of certain populations among those being pushed needs to be understood as not mere chance. People who are deemed to be inferior or defective in more than one way (e.g., being Black, female, and lesbian) have an increased likelihood of being pushed into the river.

## MULTIPLE SOCIAL IDENTITIES

In learning about the common elements of oppression, it is often assumed that because one is oppressed—such as by being gay or lesbian, being Jewish, or being a woman—this will lead people automatically toward empathy with other oppressed communities. There is a widespread belief that participation in one kind of liberating movement, such as feminism or gay rights, leads automatically to antiracism. This is not the case and we need to understand why it isn't. Understanding the dynamics of oppression in the current historical and political context involves seeing how oppressive systems operate to "divide and conquer" oppressed populations from each other. It also means understanding the dynamics of internalized oppression, whereby persons may celebrate a part of their acceptable social identity while denigrating their own devalued, unacceptable part(s).

Everyone has multiple social identities based on race, ethnicity, gender, sexual orientation, ability, class, and/or other factors. Thus, most people are both targets and agents of oppression (Bell, 1997). While people may be vulnerable to being pushed into the river based on one aspect of their social identity, the same people may push others into the river based on a diverse social identity. The secret of privilege gets complicated as one aspect of an individual's identity may confer unmerited privilege while, at the same time, another aspect of that same person's identity creates disadvantages.

Most people are uncomfortable when multiple identities are examined within a framework of power and privilege. Privilege is nice to have, and people don't want to notice it if it might mean having to give it up. When power and privilege are threatened, attempts are made to hold on to them. As the population of the United States becomes more diverse, White Americans are becoming nervous about losing their dominant position, as evidenced by an alarming increase in acts of overt and sometimes violent racism. Males are often uncomfortable with the transition from their dominant gender status to participating with more equity in relationships with women, and they will find covert and overt ways to hang on to their gender privilege, while not appearing to do so. Too many segments of the heterosexual population remain committed to their position of dominance. This is evidenced by a willingness to defend and legitimize heterosexual privilege, oppose legalization of marriage between gays and lesbians, and even justify hate crimes in the name of God. Most people who enjoy economic advantage do not even consider the possibility of giving up their position of dominance and privilege or supporting policies that would make accumulation of wealth possible for everyone. Justifications for an unequal class structure remain deeply embedded in the collective psyche of the United States.

Even while the world is rapidly changing, the reality of the deep-seated commitment to dominance, power, and privilege by those who have it strongly suggests that a peaceful transition to a new kind of America, in which no group is in a dominant position, will not be easy. The transition to a just and equitable society will require considerable change in education and personal values. It will require deep psychological shifts for all. Those in dominant positions must deal with overestimation of self based on the internalization of the myth of meritocracy. Those in subordinate positions must deal with underestimation of self and how negative stereotypes are internalized and can lead to a lack of challenging societal and institutional constraints. The challenge of promoting and developing social work practice that emphasizes a social justice perspective and the associated profession change is the work of culturally competent practice. That challenge leads to a central question: What must take place in the lives of White people, of males, of heterosexuals, of economically advantaged people, of able people, of young people, for them to see that now is the time to begin their journey from dominance to diversity—from marginalizing others through dismissive attitudes and exclusion to inclusion? What issues must be addressed in the current practice climate if social work is to play an effective role in such change?

The next exercise is aimed at helping you to explore issues related to your own multiple identities, power, and privilege.

## Transformative Learning Processes

We have presented several concepts in this chapter and have raised several challenging questions. These questions require attention in your own personal journey as you engage in learning about diversity for social justice. As was stated in the introduction to this book, a major transformation is ultimately called for at the level of a paradigmatic shift in one's way of thinking about difference that appreciates difference and thus diminishes and even

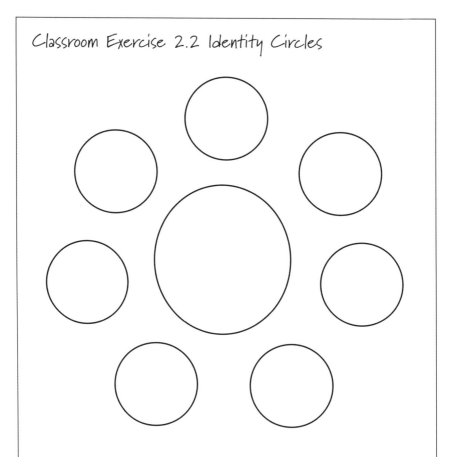

Classroom Exercise 2.2 Identity Circles

Write your name in the center circle and respond to the question: "Who am I?" by filling in the other circles with other identities that you consider to be important to your sense of self.

Be specific, for example, write woman or female and not gender. Students break into pairs to share their profiles and discuss their answers to the following questions:

• Which identity feels most primary to you? Why?

• What dominant group identities surface in your discussion that you did not include?

Share your thoughts about your impressions of what you wrote.

extinguishes the exercise of domination and power based on difference. Facilitating such a major shift requires a continuous quest to grasp and understand what is involved in the *process* of learning, even when engaged in it. The process of constructing antiracist, antisexist, antiheterosexist, anticlassist, antiageist identity, consciousness, and behavior is a transformative rather than a linear process. In other words, it is a process that is influenced by multiple factors that challenge one's sense of self and basis of self-esteem. It is a process that can take unpredictable twists and turns rather than proceeding in linear, sequential stages. Unexamined feelings are often aroused in the process of exploring the meaning of difference and how privilege and power are determined in relation to difference. Learning about diversity and social justice requires a willingness to confront and work through unresolved conflicts in relation to one's own role, status, and participation in an oppressive society.

As people face these learning challenges, they inevitably will uncover contradictions between the principles they verbalize and their behaviors, between inherited ideas they have been socialized into and new information, between self-image and feedback from others. And when they uncover contradictions, the search for new ways to think and act is ignited. This search motivates continued learning (Derman-Sparks & Brunson Phillips, 1997). Learning about diversity and oppression involves questioning one's assumptions and exploring alternative ideas in a spirit of critical inquiry. This is not only difficult; it is psychologically explosive (Brookfield, 1990).

People who engage in this work can expect to undergo profound changes in the process in that they find themselves moving beyond familiar points, out of their "cozy boxes."[3] They can also expect that change is inevitably coupled with substantial distress. Ultimately, the struggle for social workers requires that they develop a positive social identity for themselves to better value their clients' identities and related struggles (Pinderhughes, 1989). The struggle for a positive social identity varies, depending on one's unique experiences and backgrounds related to social status and power.

Educational frameworks that bring together cultural diversity and social justice challenge one's worldview. Personal turmoil and reevaluation are part of the process and require the development of a positive social

---

3. A term used by Sigmund Koch, University Professors Program, Boston University.

identity within a context of dominant power structures. The challenges of learning and changing can feel overwhelming at times. No one can do this work in isolation. It is too complex. It requires multiple voices in dialogue and struggle. It requires knowledge building of skills, concepts, theories, and history. It requires emotional support from people who understand its demands and can help keep the focus on growing in the midst of a lot of heat. It requires patience and gentleness—both with oneself and with one another. Finding, developing, and using peer and collegial support is needed. As one navigates the learning process, it helps to know that everyone is affected by injustice and everyone needs to be in the struggle together to find solutions.

# Conclusion

This chapter highlighted some of the issues and obstacles people may face in their journeys to develop cultural competence that is characterized by an integration of diversity and social justice. A conceptual framework was presented with four essential components aimed ultimately at eliminating oppressive systems. What is proposed is transformation on the most fundamental level of knowledge creation. What does this mean? It means exposing the ways in which implicit cultural assumptions, frames of reference, and biases within our profession influence what social workers think they know about people and their environments and the helping strategies they adopt. It means examining how knowledge is created and influenced by factors of race, ethnicity, gender, class, age, ability, and sexual orientation. It means identifying and examining the human interests and value assumptions of those who create knowledge. It means creating a learning environment that critically challenges the facts, concepts, paradigms, themes, and explanations routinely accepted in mainstream academia (Banks, 1993). In chapter 3, key concepts and definitions provide theoretical grounding for your further understanding of the complex elements comprised in cultural competence.

# References

Banks, J. A. (1993, September). Multicultural education: Development, dimensions, and challenges. *Phi Delta Kappa, 75*(1), 22–28.

Bell, L. A. (1997). Theoretical foundations for social justice education. In M. Adams, L. A. Bell, & P. Griffin (Eds.), *Teaching for diversity and social justice: A sourcebook* (pp. 3–15). New York: Routledge.

Brookfield, S. (1990). Using critical incidents to explore learners' assumptions. In J. Mezirow & Associates, *Fostering critical reflection in adulthood: A guide to transformative and emanicipatory learning* (pp. 177–198). San Francisco: Jossey-Bass.

Council on Social Work Education (1992). *Curriculum policy statements for baccalaureate degree and master's degree programs in social work education.* Alexandria, VA: Author.

Council on Social Work Education (2001). Educational policy and accreditation standards. Alexandria, VA: Author.

Derman-Sparks, L., & Brunson Phillips, C. (1997). *Teaching/learning anti-racism.* New York: Teachers College Press, Columbia University.

Edwards-Orr, M. T. (1988, March). Helping white students confront white racism. Paper presented at the Annual Program Meeting of the Council on Social Work Education, Atlanta, GA.

Frankenberg, R. (1993). *The social construction of whiteness: White women, race matters.* Minneapolis: University of Minnesota Press.

Gil, D. (1998). *Confronting injustice and oppression: Concepts and strategies for social workers.* New York: Columbia University.

Hacker, A. (1992). *Two nations: Black and white, separate, hostile, unequal.* New York: Charles Scribner's Sons.

Hopps, J. (1982). Oppression based on color (editorial). *Social Work, 27*(1), 3–5.

Howard, G. (1993). Whites in multicultural education: Rethinking our role. *Phi Delta Kappa, 75,* 36–41.

Huntington, S. (2002). *Who are we? The challenge to America's national identity.* New York, NY: Simon & Schuster.

Jensen, B. (1998, July 9). Wake up to white privilege (editorial), *Baltimore Sun.*

Knowles, L., & Prewitt, K. (1969). *Institutional racism in America.* Englewood Cliffs, NJ: Prentice-Hall.

Lipsitz. G. (1998). *The possessive investment in Whiteness: How White people profit from identity politics.* Philadelphia: Temple University Press.

McIntosh, P. (1995). White privilege and male privilege: A personal account of coming to see correspondences through work in women's studies. In M. L. Andersen and P. H. Collins, *Race, class, and gender: An anthology* (pp. 76–87). New York: Wadsworth.

Omi, M., & Winant, H. (1986). *Racial formation in the United States from the 1960's to the 1980's.* New York: Routledge.

Pinderhughes, E. (1989). *Understanding race, ethnicity, and power: The key to efficacy in clinical practice.* New York: Macmillan.

Schlesinger, A. (1991). *The disunity of America: Reflections on a multicultural society.* New York, NY: W. W. Norton & Company.

Wijeyesinghe, C. L., Griffin, P., & Love, B. (1997). Racism curriculum design. In M. Adams, L. A. Bell, & P. Griffin, *Teaching for diversity and social justice: A sourcebook* (p. 90). New York: Routledge.

# Chapter Three
# Key Concepts and Definitions

In the first chapter, we focused on understanding social justice, and in the second chapter we presented a conceptual framework for understanding culturally competent social work practice that by necessity integrates diversity and social justice. We also highlighted some of the barriers social workers face in their journey toward culturally competency.

In this chapter we present definitions of cultural diversity and multiculturalism; racism, prejudice, discrimination, power, and privilege; structural and interpersonal dynamics of oppression; and cultural competence. We emphasize the significance of self-awareness and the role of *historical context, lived experience, and social power* in understanding the experiences of others, particularly as they affect social, ethnic, and racial identity.[1]

Empowerment and social movement activities and events relevant to particular groups are outlined to illuminate significant historical factors and to stimulate thinking about strength-based practice at multiple levels with individuals, families, groups, communities, and organizations.

# Cultural Diversity and Multiculturalism

## Cultural Diversity

Cultural competence is about effective engagement and provision of services to diverse populations. The definition of cultural diversity that we offer focuses on differences among groups that signify distinctive characteristics, social identity, and, depending on the diversity, contribute to a greater or lesser degree to their culture. These differences include ethnicity, gender,

---

1. Previous chapters point out that we treat "race" as a social construction and refer to "race" as an identity based on values, beliefs, and life experience. We recognize that, societally, phenotype is viewed as representing real genetic and biological differences between "races," for which there is no evidence.

age, sexual orientation, religion, ability, and socioeconomic class. Diversity is inseparable from issues of oppression and social and economic justice. Both diversity and social justice perspectives recognize the historical and ongoing oppression and privilege that different social identity groups experience in society. A diversity perspective acknowledges that members of some groups enjoy privileges and higher status, while other groups are relegated to lower positions in society. It recognizes socioeconomic class as a primary element of oppression. In fact, it sees the creation and maintenance of a class system based on difference as a function of oppression. The approach presented here also highlights the reality that most people identify with not just one but several cultural groups. These multiple social identities play out in various ways in people's lives. In other words, everyone's experience can be characterized by vulnerability to harm in some situations and by privileged status in other situations.

An increasingly diverse population characterizes most corners of 21st-century American life, in both urban and rural settings, with diverse ethnicity already representing 30% of the American population. While diversity is most salient in relation to ethnicity, it is much broader than national origin and culture. It also refers to uniqueness in the lives of individuals, families, and communities based on socioeconomic class, gender, sexual orientation, and disability, to name a few. Diversity is often viewed as divergence from the "norm" that is embodied in dominant culture, and the term is understood in relation to being "different" from dominant cultural values, beliefs, practices, and phenotype, that is, how one looks. However, this view colludes in marginalizing diverse individuals and obscures the reality that the phenomenon is based on the privilege of the dominant group to define and name. For example, the term *Oriental*, in the past used to refer to Asians, assumes the "center" to be Europe, and "orientals" to reside east of Europe, rather than using the name that Asians choose for themselves. From a social justice perspective, diversity is viewed as "difference between individuals" rather than the "other," which upholds dominance and social power in a segment of society rather than distributing these across all groups and classes.

Along with the increased visibility of alternatives to the dominant cultural belief system, we are seeing an increase in value judgments, negative stereotyping, and reductionist thinking. Reductionist thinking seeks to explain complex situations by looking to a single aspect or part to explain the whole. This kind of thinking characterizes what is currently referred to as societal "culture wars." There is a greater urgency for professional social workers, in this climate, to develop and use critical thinking skills to identify assumptions found in reductionist thinking and negative stereotypes. A willingness to examine existing evidence and open dialogue supports critical thinking and exposes the myopic, shortsighted thinking that often underlies the value judgments directed at diversity.

The significance and impact of these concepts in the everyday life of all persons, not just those identified as "diverse," may not be obvious at first. Yet, discussions about difference and diversity almost predictably evoke intense feelings and typically become conversational lightning rods. Such intense reactions suggest that diversity issues set off emotions and concerns that matter immensely to people. However, rather than exploring one's biases and beliefs, the more typical response pattern is to make judgments about those who are "different," which effectively interferes with open dialogue.

Another typical phenomenon is a lack of motivation on the part of many individuals to explore their own unique, diverse national origins, even as they contribute richness to their social identity. The reasons for this are undoubtedly varied and somewhat speculative. However, depending on one's relationship to the dominant culture, a variety of conflicts that create discomfort about exploring one's background may be experienced. We present here three experiences that we have encountered with students to help you explore your position vis-à-vis exploring your own unique identity:

1. If your social identity benefits by validation and recognition from the dominant culture, you may have a sense of not having a specific "culture" with which to identify. However, close scrutiny of day-to-day practices, holidays that are honored, and celebrations in which your family participates illuminate cultural beliefs and values that organize your life experiences.

2. If you identify more strongly with a "traditional, ethnic" culture, you often may encounter experiences in which your culture is disparaged by the dominant culture. For example, a teacher may have insisted to your parents that they should stop speaking their native language with

you as a child, rather than exploring ways of maintaining your native language and simultaneously mastering English.

3. If you have multiple ethnic backgrounds, you may find that you are not comfortable categorizing your social identity as being of one culture; you may identify with several cultures. You may feel challenged to develop a perspective for yourself that honors all the facets of your identity, while others seem to insist on identifying you with only one facet.

The following classroom exercise is aimed at helping you to reflect on and share with others your social identity and cultural identifications.

---

*Classroom Exercise 3.1*
*Creating Your Cultural Chest*

Prepare a chest filled with symbolic cultural treasures such as religious or ethnic artifacts that represent who you are. Decorate the outside of the chest to represent what you let others see of who you are. Bring your chest to class, where you will present it to others as a means to tell them who you are.

As an alternative to actually preparing a chest, you might imagine what you would put into such a chest and how you would decorate the outside. You may then share with others in class by describing your "virtual" chest.

*Debriefing Questions:*

1. What feelings did this exercise trigger in you?
2. What was your experience in doing this?
3. What connections did you make, if any, with your life experiences?
4. What learning do you take from this activity?

---

The purpose of the following self-reflection paper is to provide an opportunity for you to explore your ethnic/racial roots and examine the unique experiences of significant individuals who have shaped your path in life. This exercise emphasizes that learning about diversity and dealing with it is about: 1) taking responsibility to explore how you have benefited from the institutionalization of racism and oppression or have been a target of these, 2) engaging in examination of how these have affected your identity, and 3) determining in what ways you can engage in change strategies to do away with oppressive structures.

**REFLECTION EXERCISE 3.1 ETHNIC ROOTS PAPER**

The purpose of this assignment is to explore your ethnic/racial roots and examine the unique experiences of your parents/grandparents/great-grandparents and beyond/or other significant individuals who have shaped your path in life. The paper should be 6–7 pages and respond to the following set of questions:

**A** Background: Very briefly describe yourself (age, birthplace, socioeconomic class and status when you were growing up, current cultural identification[s], etc.)

**B** Background of Parents/Grandparents/Great-Grandparents, and so on

- A description of what you know about your (1) mother, (2) father, (3) maternal grandparents, (3) paternal grandparents, (4) maternal and paternal great-grandparents, and so on. If you are adopted, consider either your birth parents or adoptive parents in your response—whichever best fits your sense of identity.

- If your ancestors immigrated to the United States, how did they enter (e.g., were they voluntary immigrants, involuntary through conquest, time period of entry, etc.)? If they were not immigrants, what was their experience with the imposition of the U.S. political system?

**C** Experiences With White Conformity and Factors Affecting Inclusion

- By the standards of the dominant White culture, were individuals related to you included in or excluded from American society?

**REFLECTION EXERCISE 3.1 ETHNIC ROOTS PAPER (continued)**

- How did they avoid/attempt/achieve assimilation and integration? How did they attempt to be or resist being accepted by the dominant culture (e.g., Were names changed to fit into mainstream American society? Were ethnic roots emphasized or downplayed? Were traditions/language/customs suppressed or passed down through the generations?)?

- What role did social class and social power play in their experiences?

**D** Conclusion

- What conclusions do you draw about your own current identity based on your ethnic roots, socialization, and personal experiences?

- How have you benefited from or been a target of racism and oppression based on your ethnic roots?

- What responsibility do you feel today to engage in change strategies based on your own identity and ethnic roots?

# Multiculturalism

We use the term *multiculturalism* in relation to issues of representation and democratic inclusiveness. Multiculturalism must be understood in the context of sociopolitical power and a historical past and present where racist exclusions have been and are "calculated, brutally rational, and profitable" (Goldberg, 1993, p. 105). This perspective on multicultural practice emphasizes a goal of teaching social workers to "interrogate, challenge, and transform those cultural practices that sustain racism" and to "link the struggle for inclusion with relations of power in the broader society" (Giroux, 2000, p. 499).

A multicultural society means change, not status quo. Diversity has always been a fundamental characteristic of American life. However, there is now increased awareness of its presence, due in part to immigration, growth of diverse populations, and greater media attention to diversity-related concerns. Demographic predictions forecast an America composed of a variety of ethnic and multiethnic individuals and populations that will characterize different geographic regions within the next few decades. Demographic changes enrich communities through the introduction of new immigrant groups, greater integration of diverse cultural contributions (e.g., food, music, art) into the mainstream culture, and increased inclusion of diverse groups into different aspects of community and professional settings due to their upward mobility. Through increased interaction with those different from ourselves, old perceptions and attitudes are challenged, and, in the best of circumstances, new thinking and behaviors are stimulated. To stand still in this ever-changing context is to go backward.

In the next classroom exercise you are asked to reflect on your social identity profile and address the different social groups with which you identify. In relation to each possible group, make a check in the column to the right, and in the third column (status) describe your identification (e.g., Latino, female, low-income, Buddhist). Feel free to list as many associations as you make with any one social identity.

Shifts in roles and interaction stimulated by demographic social changes have created ambiguous situations that require more interpersonal negotiation than one customarily faces in familiar interactions. While this may be demanding and stressful, it also increases the potential for developing new interpersonal skills that are essential for engaging in diverse interactions. By legitimizing difference as something that is to be appreciated and understood, processes are activated that can lead to increased awareness of one's own value system and behavior in relation to others. When there is curiosity and risk taking, interactions with unfamiliar individuals in new settings can be successful and rewarding and can result in new connections. They can stimulate new reactions related to dealing with one's own identity, what one values, and motivation to know others different from ourselves. In the presence of diversity, the rules for interaction change, and the possibility of gaining understanding of different perspectives is enhanced. This qualitative change in one's interactions with others and the social settings in which we find ourselves can provide unique feedback that fosters curiosity about others and the development of personal and

*Classroom Exercise 3.2*
*Social Group Membership Profile\**

| Social Identities | Examples of Social Group Memberships |
|---|---|
| Race | Black, Asian, White, Latino/a, Native American, Biracial, Pacific Islander |
| Gender | male, female, transgender |
| Class | poor, low income, working class, owning class |
| Physical/Mental Developmental Ability | able, disabled |
| Sexual Orientation | lesbian, gay, bisexual, heterosexual, asexual, transgender, questioning |
| Religion | Christian, Jewish, Protestant, Buddhist, Muslim, Hindu |
| Age | transitional youth, young adult, midlife adult, elderly adult |

**Personal Social Group Membership Profile**

| Social Identities | Membership | Status |
|---|---|---|
| Race | | |
| Gender | | |
| Class | | |
| Age | | |
| Sexual Orientation | | |
| Religion | | |
| Ability/Disability | | |

*Adapted from Adams, Bell, & Griffin (1997).

professional awareness of self. We suggest you do the following self-reflection exercise as a way to explore the value of curiosity and risk taking as you consider self-disclosure about your own cultural identity.

**REFLECTION EXERCISE 3.2  SELF-REFLECTION**

1. What would someone who didn't know you at all learn about you if he or she were to learn about the historical context of your culture and your family life experiences?

2. What would you look for in that person's interaction with you that would tell you this is someone with whom you want to dialogue?

3. What would be missed or made invisible about you, that is important to you, if friends did not take the time to get to know you?

4. Given what you know is important for you about your cultural identification and family life experiences, what questions does this evoke for you about the experiences of others who are different from you?

Bridging differences leads us into new experiential terrain requiring a combination of emotional and intellectual work. It involves active engagement and negotiation with others whose communication and interaction styles are different from one's own style. It is easy to be seduced into using initial impressions and knowledge about diverse groups in a boilerplate fashion as if unfamiliar cultures were static or all individuals within that group were homogeneous. It is tempting for social workers to want to know the "five things that we need to know to work with a particular population." However, it is essential to treat new information about diverse groups as hypotheses that continually need to be matched to current interactions. Then ongoing interactions and impressions are viewed as a basis for the development of more complex knowledge about other individuals and cultural groups. In summary, the new multicultural demographics of society require change and adaptation. Individuals will succeed to the degree that they can process their own experience, value diversity, and sustain a robust curiosity about their experiences with others. We suggest you engage in the following exercise and complete the assignment to experience the life of a person from a cultural group different from your own.

Classroom Exercise 3.3
Immersion "Shadow" Experience

The purpose of this exercise is to provide you with the opportunity to observe and experience the life of a person from a cultural group different from your own. It will also allow you to reflect on the similarities and differences between your own cultural group and another cultural group.

Select a person from a culture different from your own who is willing to allow you to be present at five different events in his or her life. The person must also be willing to have candid discussions with you about his or her life experiences and the impact of the person's culture on those experiences. The person selected must not be a friend or acquaintance whom you have known for more than one month. The *three to five events* in the person's life that you will "shadow" are as follows:

1. You will participate in a *family meal* in the person's home.
2. You will participate in a *family special event*, such as a birthday/ anniversary party, wedding, graduation, coming of age, etc.
3. You will attend a *spiritual/religious event* or discussion about the person's spiritual/religious life (e.g., baptism, bar mitzvah, Ramadan, Purim).
4. You will observe the person in his or her *workplace*.
5. You will attend a *recreational/leisure activity* with the person.

Reflection Paper

At the end of each event, write a two-page *Reflection Paper* on the experience. By the end of your 3–5 events spent with your person, you will have 6–10 pages as *the core of your Reflection Paper.* Your reflection on each event should be no more than 2 pages long and should include the following:

- •Observations about the interactions among the people participating in the event.
- •Your comfort level at the event and the group's comfort level with your presence.
- •Similarities to and differences from your own life experiences.
- •Myths, stereotypes, biases, and prejudices that you had about the person's cultural group that were challenged as a result of your experience at the events.
- •Impact of the experience on your personal and professional life.

*Debriefing Questions:*

1. What feelings were triggered in you as you did this exercise?
2. What was your experience in doing this?
3. What connections did you make, if any, with your life experiences?
4. What learning do you take from this activity?

# Racism, Prejudice, and Discrimination Related to Power and Privilege

A primary premise of this book is that culturally competent social work involves effective interventions with diverse clients coupled with a commitment to promote social justice. This perspective begins with a focus on racism because of its entrenchment in the history and character of the United States and its formative role in disenfranchising and marginalizing significant portions of the population. We view racism above all as a sociopolitical phenomenon that is characterized by social power. Its attitudinal (i.e., thoughts, feelings, and behaviors) and interpersonal manifestations vary in relation to one's social power.

# Racism

Racism is defined as the "generalization, institutionalization and assignment of values to real or imaginary differences between people in order to justify a state of privilege, aggression, and/or violence" (Bulhan, 1985, p. 13). As one form of oppression, racism is "a mode of human relations involving domination and exploitation—economic, social and psychological" (Gil, 1998, p. 10). As a form of domination, racism is a means to exploit so that one socioeconomic class benefits from another's resources and capacities, for example, through its labor (Gil, 1998). This suggests that social, economic, and political forces determine the social status of racial groups based on the meaning of difference that determines social categories (Omi & Winant, 1986).

We view institutional racism as business as usual, premised on economic and technocratic means that do not require "psychological mediation" (Kovel, 1984, p. xi) or intent to discriminate. This leads to discriminatory behaviors based on merely implementing commonly accepted policies and practices. Social workers need to focus on the sociopolitical dynamics that result from power and privilege on both psychological and institutional levels to be prepared to intervene on all levels: intrapersonal, interpersonal, and institutional.

# Prejudice and Discrimination

Prejudice and discrimination are distinct from racism. Prejudice refers to prejudgments or ungrounded adverse opinion or beliefs about others (Blumenfeld & Raymond, 2000). Psychological explanations about prejudice frequently focus on how it represents projection of one's unowned and unacceptable personal qualities onto people who are targets of oppression (Allport, 1954; Lichtenberg, van Beusekom, & Gibbons, 1997). Because the origins of prejudice "include both the psychological makeup of the individual and the structural organization of society" (Blumenfeld & Raymond, 2000, p. 26), the sociopolitical and ideological context within which individuals are socialized plays a powerful role in shaping negative stereotypes about target groups (Garcia-Bahne, 1981). These negative stereotypes can survive, even in the face of discrediting evidence.

Discrimination represents an action intended to have a "differential and/or harmful effect on members" of a group (Pincus, 2000, p. 31), and it has been characterized as a response that creates distance, separation, exclusion, and devaluation (Lott, 2002). Pincus (2000) suggests that individual and institutional discrimination represent behavioral and policy actions that are intended to have a harmful effect, whereas structural discrimination refers to policies and behaviors that may be neutral in intent yet have negative, harmful consequences on target groups. *When discrimination is buttressed by social power it represents racism and oppression. When it is not backed by social power, biased behaviors represent individual discriminatory actions. As such, the intention of discriminatory behavior is not significant, what matters is understanding the context in which it occurs and the impact it has on individuals, families, and communities.*

Learning about racism facilitates learning about other oppressions such as sexism, classism, ableism, and heterosexism. While racism has primacy in American life based on the heritage of slavery, genocide, colonization, and exploitation,[2] cultural competence must include awareness of other diversities and oppressions. In racism, where one facet of an individual having to do with phenotype (e.g., hair texture, skin color, facial features, physiology) is taken as the whole of the individual; likewise with the other "isms"; one facet of an individual such as gender, sexual orientation, or ability is also presumed to be all that a person is. One's entire being is viewed in one-dimensional, monolithic terms.

Developing the ability to "walk in the shoes of the other" and suspend one's own perspective, as part of learning about the worldviews of others, is one of the most significant aspects of culturally competent practice.

Although it is important to learn about diverse cultures, a core skill in cross-cultural competence is the skill and ability to engage with others for the purpose of developing a working relationship. It is then that we can learn about others' meanings, values, and beliefs. Awareness and ability to empathize need to be developed within the context of the cultural, social, and legal realities and the unique patterns of domination associated with each "ism," while keeping perspective on how power and privilege are

---

2. The experience of African Americans, Latinos, American Indians, and Asians at formative periods of this country's development has been rife with domination and subjugation based on fortifying political and economic interests.

manifested within each of them (Wildman & Davis, 2000). Just as the system of White privilege based on an advantage of race limits access to resources and decision making linked to full participation in society for those considered to be White and limits access for those not identified as White, a system of privilege operates in similar ways based on other factors such as gender, sexual orientation, or ability (McIntosh, 1989; Tatem, 2000).

# Structural and Interpersonal Dynamics of Oppression

By understanding oppression and racism, we shed light on the sociopolitical conditions that intensify reactions to difference and often lead to moralizing and placing blame. An understanding of the dynamics of oppression reveals how factors related to individual characteristics often become overrated, and contextual factors, such as socioeconomic class, privilege, entitlement, negative stereotyping, and marginalization, remain unnoticed. By being aware of oppression and racism, we are able to develop a balanced view that factors in both contextual and individual factors. When we look only at an individual's choices as a way of explaining his or her difficulties (e.g., substance abuse, domestic violence, homelessness), we risk "blaming the victim." On the other hand, glossing over individual factors by looking only at environmental, historical, and situational factors as a way of explaining behavior is disempowering, since it assumes that individual effort is ineffective in dealing with those obstacles. The key is to inquire about the match between needs and resources, that is, to determine to what degree the requisite resources and supports are present for the individual to exercise self-determination.

## Oppression

Issues of power and privilege related to social identities must be understood within the context of oppression. Oppression is defined as a situation in which one segment of the population acts to prevent another segment from attaining access to resources or acts to inhibit or devalue them to dominate them (Bulhan, 1985). Young (2000) suggests that oppression is not based on any one group membership and, as a means of distinguishing among various experiences, identifies "five faces" of oppression: exploitation, marginalization, powerlessness, cultural imperialism, and violence. The five dynamics are intended to provide a means to recognize the variety of ways that different groups experience oppression. They help us to avoid hierarchical comparisons about who is most oppressed. These concepts assist in explaining how devaluation and invisibility become part of the experience of oppression. Young emphasizes that the presence of any of these five experiences or faces constitutes oppression, and that most people experience some combination of these.

## Common Elements of Oppression

There are elements common to all oppressions regardless of the target population (Pharr, 1988). First, oppression always bestows power and advantage on certain people who are regarded as the norm and denies power and advantage to others based on their status as "other" or different. The defined norm (i.e., White, male, heterosexual) is the standard of *rightness* against which all "others" are judged; the "other" (i.e., not White, not male, not heterosexual) is not only different from the norm, but is also believed and perceived to be inferior and deviant, which then justifies conferring advantage on those who fit the norm and disadvantaging the "other."

There is an important distinction between social and individual power. Racism, sexism, and heterosexism are sociopolitical phenomena and not personal prejudices based on individual power and stereotypes. There is a difference between talking about prejudice and discrimination (personal power) and talking about a system of advantage that confers economic, social, judicial, and political (social) power on people who fit the "norm." To understand oppression, we can look at indicators and patterns in institutional practices and policies. For example, in the political arena, how many U.S. senators are Black, Latino, female, or openly homosexual? In relation to economic indicators, who is represented disproportionately among those who are poor? The chart below highlights some key events that illustrate how institutional policies and practices have historically conferred power and access to resources to those in the dominant society (i.e., Whites) by denying power and access to resources to those deemed to be outside the "norm" (i.e., non-White). It illustrates impressively how racism is an institutionalized sociopolitical phenomenon based on a social system of power and advantage that is distinct from personal prejudice based on individual power and stereotypes.

A second element common to all types of oppression is that the various types of oppression are held in place by ideology and violence or the threat of violence. The ideology on which racial oppression is based is that of superiority based on race (i.e., White supremacy). Likewise, the ideology on which sexual oppression is based is that of superiority based on gender (i.e., male), and the basis for homosexual oppression is an ideology of superiority based on sexual orientation (i.e., heterosexuality). Violence, which is used to enforce and maintain all oppressions, comes in many forms and may be physical and direct (e.g., lynching, rape, battering, gay bashing) or personal and psychological (e.g., name-calling based on dominant ideology and negative stereotypes). Violence may be indirect and/or institutionalized. For example, it may be associated with high poverty rates, the predominance of men of color in the criminal justice system and on death row, and the reality of police brutality.

A third common element of all oppression is that it is *institutionalized.* This means that racism, sexism, and heterosexism are built into the norms, traditions, laws, and policies of a society, so that even those who have nonracist, nonsexist, and nonheterosexist beliefs are compelled to act in accordance with institutional interests, that is, "business as usual."

Institutionalized racism, specifically, ensures White entitlement and benefits regardless of the intentions of individuals in those institutions (see Chart 3.1 for a powerful illustration of the power of institutionalized racism historically). According to Pinderhughes (1989), institutional racism ensures that Whites benefit, exonerates them from responsibility, and sanctions the blaming of people of color for those restrictions and limitations imposed by oppression. She points out that there is considerable resistance to comprehending the institutional aspect of racism and that the process of understanding its systemic nature can be very painful. This is especially the case for White people, who see themselves as different from Whites whom they view as racists. Pinderhughes writes about how particularly devastating it is for White people who have been involved in civil rights activities to face the implication that they, along with other Whites, are the beneficiaries of racism. There is a sense of injury that stems from recognition of themselves as trapped in the systemic process of racism that benefits them and exploits people of color. This sense of injury is exacerbated further by the realization that, while for many people of color this reality has been obvious, for Whites this has been obscure.

---

**CHART 3.1**
**RACIST INSTITUTIONAL PRACTICES AND POLICIES:**
**KEY EVENTS IN THE UNITED STATES, 1819–1942***

| | |
|---|---|
| 1819 | Congress passes "civilization act" to assimilate Native Americans |
| 1830 | Congress passes Indian removal act |
| 1831–38 | Indian tribes resettled in West in Trail of Tears |
| 1848 | Treaty of Guadalupe Hidalgo cedes Mexican territory in Southwest to the United States |
| 1857 | *Dred Scott v. Sanford* endorses southern views on race and territories |
| 1865 | President Johnson begins Reconstruction; Confederate leaders regain power; White southern governments pass restrictive Black codes |
| 1882 | Congress prohibits Chinese immigration for 10 years |
| 1883 | Supreme Court strikes down 1875 Civil Rights Act |
| 1887 | Dawes Act dissolves tribal lands and grants land allotments to individual families |
| 1890 | Wounded Knee massacre; final suppression of Plains tribes by U.S. Army |
| 1896 | *Plessy v. Ferguson* upholds doctrine of "separate but equal" among Blacks and Whites in public facilities |
| 1899 | *Cummins v. County Board of Education* applies "separate but equal" doctrine to public schools |
| 1902 | Congress excludes Chinese immigration indefinitely |
| 1914 | U.S. troops invade Mexico during Mexican Revolution |
| 1923 | Ku Klux Klan activity peaks |
| 1931 | Nine African American men arrested in Scottsboro affair |
| 1942 | 120,000 Japanese Americans sent to relocation camps |

---

*Adapted from Adams, Bell, & Griffin (1997, pp. 105–106).

Another common element of oppression is the invisibility endured by groups who are oppressed. By keeping the oppression structurally invisible, individuals and groups are socially defined in a way that inhibits recognition of the group's heterogeneity by the dominant group. In addition, the internalization of external sociopolitical judgments that devalue aspects of one's identity inevitably leads to individuals undervaluing and ignoring substantive parts of their own origins and history. These issues are addressed in a later section and specifically deal with how, on an interpersonal level, the invisibility and exclusion in part is buttressed through moral exclusion.

The issue of multiple identities further complicates the dynamics of oppression. Individual conditions of oppression often involve a convergence between aspects of one's experience where one is a target of oppression (e.g., as a low-income, disabled female, a Latina, an African American, a gay woman) with other aspects of one's experience as privileged (e.g., a middle- or high-income gay person, a disabled Euro-American male) (Rose, 2002). Understanding the presence of power, privilege, advantage, or constraints introduced through oppression in one's life draws attention to experiences and realities that may have been denied or minimized and lays the foundation for connecting with others different from oneself. For example, a gay White male who is in the process of accepting his sexuality and is not "out" may exercise his White privilege out of awareness without recognizing that until he begins to deal with social power issues in the process of resolving his identity and when he more thoroughly decides to manage his identity. Or someone whose phenotype is stereotypically Euro-American, and has another less socially valued heritage, may choose to underplay the latter until that person has resolved and integrated his or her social identity. The next exercise provides you with an opportunity to explore your own identities in relation to power and privilege.

## Moral Exclusion

The concept of moral exclusion explains how exclusionary behavior is promoted and maintained on an interpersonal level. Moral exclusion refers to the process of placing those who are different from oneself or one's group outside the boundaries of fair treatment by invoking assumptions about who deserves just treatment and who should enjoy society's benefits

## MULTIPLE IDENTITIES: POWER AND NONPOWER

Take all of the identities that you wrote in Reflection Exercise 2.5 in chapter 2 and categorize them in the chart below. For your identities that are seen as "superior," "normal," or "the best group to be in" by the norms of dominant society, place that identity in the first column. For your identities that are seen as "inferior," "disadvantaged," "discriminated against," or "needing help" by the norms of dominant society, place that identity in the second column. Reflect on your profile as a person with many identities. Which aspects of who you are confer privilege and power? Which aspects do not?

| Aspects of My Identity That Confer Privilege and Power and Are Seen as Dominant | Aspects of My Identity That Do Not Confer Privilege or Power and Are Seen as Subordinate |
| --- | --- |
|  |  |
|  |  |
|  |  |
|  |  |
|  |  |

(Deutsch, 1990). The concept of moral exclusion presumes that some individuals or populations are subordinate in their level of development on moral, intellectual, or spiritual grounds. This rationalization becomes the basis of exclusion that goes beyond interpersonal interaction through its social and economic consequences of marginalization and exclusion. Persons outside one's moral boundaries are seen as expendable or undeserving, so

Classroom Exercise 3.4
Exploring Your Moral Boundaries

Imagine that the circle below represents your moral boundaries. List the individuals or groups you believe deserve just treatment and should enjoy society's benefits inside the circle. Place the names of the individuals or groups you believe should not enjoy some of society's benefits or just treatment outside the circle. For those listed outside the circle that represents your moral boundaries, note your rationale for their exclusion (e.g., moral, intellectual, spiritual reasons). In addition, note which benefits or rights to which you believe they should not be entitled. In some cases, you may believe that they should not be entitled to some benefits and should be entitled to others; in those instances, be sure to note your beliefs and your rationale for each. For example, some people believe that gay and lesbian individuals should not enjoy the benefit of marriage (outside the circle) but should not be discriminated against in the workplace (inside the circle). Another example might be the belief that people with severe disabilities should not be allowed to marry, vote, or live independently (outside the circle).

*Questions for Reflection:*

1. Look at who is inside your circle. What is your life experience with these individuals and groups? How similar to or different from you are they? What messages did you get about each as you were growing up and from whom? What messages do you get today from people around you and from the media? Are there people inside the circle today who would not have been there in the past? What changed?

2. Look at who is outside your circle. What is your life experience with these individuals and groups? How similar to or different from you are they? What messages did you get about each as you were growing up and from whom? What messages do you get today from people around you and from the media? Are there people outside the circle today who would have been inside in the past? What changed?

3. When you look at the individuals or groups outside your circle of moral boundaries, imagine that they are clients and you are their social worker. What are the implications for practice?

*Debriefing Questions:*

1. What feelings were triggered in you as you did this exercise?
2. What was your experience in doing this?
3. What connections did you make, if any, with your life experiences?
4. What learning do you take from this activity?

harming them appears to be acceptable, appropriate, benign, or just. The process of categorizing groups negatively and excluding them from the realm of acceptable norms or values is linked to stereotypes and prejudicial attitudes related to ethnocentrism. Persons who have been and are excluded from the realm of the norms and values of social justice include people of color, women, gay/lesbian/bisexual/transgender persons, people with disabilities, poor people, and others.

There is a considerable body of literature on moral exclusion, disen-
gagement practices that make it possible to justify exclusion, and antidotes
to exclusion (Opotow, 1990). Thus, the concept of moral exclusion provides a
useful framework for helping us to understand ourselves and our beliefs in
relation to different groups in society. While seldom conscious of them, we
all have beliefs about which people should be treated justly, and the broad-
ness or narrowness of our moral boundaries is influenced by prevailing cultural norms. For example, it is no longer considered acceptable in the United
States to own people as slaves or to make interracial marriages illegal, but it
is generally considered acceptable to exclude gay men and lesbians from
certain benefits such as partner benefits and the right to marry. The identification and exclusion of an out group from the norms of fairness is a cognitive, affective, and behavioral phenomenon that enables otherwise consider-
ate people to engage in self-serving behavior or inaction in everyday situations to gain benefits, even at injurious costs to others.

The concept of moral exclusion provides a tool for making obvious
one's own personal processes of excluding certain people from the boundaries of fairness and provides a viable framework for grappling with
addressing diversity and racism within social work practice settings. The
next exercise seeks to help you to analyze your own moral boundaries with
the goal of broadening the boundaries of your social work practice to make
it consistent with cultural competency principles.

## How Oppression Is Maintained

DeRosa (1988) describes oppression as initiated and maintained at four levels encompassing individual, interpersonal, institutional, and ideological
dynamics. Maintaining oppression requires all of these levels working
together; thus, it is important to understand each level's integral contribu-
tion. The institutional level is a critical component in that it is at that level
that the societal power of discriminatory policies and practices is implemented both with awareness and out of awareness, intentionally and unintentionally. The four levels summarized by DeRosa (1988) complement
Pharr's (1988) observations on the commonalities shared by all oppressions
that were presented earlier.

*Individual level: Negative stereotypes are internalized.* Socialization into a dominant culture that values some groups and not others leads everyone, regardless of background, to internalize negative stereotypes. This happens throughout life experiences with families, friends, mentors, media, and other sources. The result is an overriding one-dimensional portrayal of diverse groups that takes one facet of a group and makes it the whole rather than recognizing complexity. As a result of socialization, attitudes are influenced to the point that one believes those one-dimensional portrayals. This affects how individuals think and feel about themselves and others.

This internalization of stereotypes creates discomfort when we engage with others different from ourselves. Either through omission or commission, it is possible to go along with the negative stereotyping. For individuals to whom the negative stereotyping is directed, the resulting criticism and judgment of one's own cultural group creates self-conflict. Racial identity theory, discussed in chapter 4, addresses how awareness of the discrepancy between internalized beliefs and personal observation prompts individuals toward exploration and change. For example, recognition that not all gays are in unstable, brief relationships or that people with disabilities lead fully developed, productive lives or that people on welfare have quality-of-life goals that are the same as other family systems, one is moved to ask why. That is the beginning of change. The following exercise illustrates how an experience with a group of people different from oneself disrupts internalized beliefs about that group.

*Interpersonal level: group activity and interpersonal interaction.* Patterns of interactions and behaviors with other people are influenced by institutions and are supported by family, peers, and the community. Through conventions of language, terminology, and ideas, negative stereotypes can be maintained through these interactions. This is poignantly illustrated by the experiences of some students when they return home from college for the holidays after being exposed to new experiences with diverse groups and become aware of the intensity of family prejudices, sometimes for the first time. This creates conflict between what they were taught and what they are now experiencing.

## Classroom Exercise 3.5   Case Vignette

As an assignment to participate in an unfamiliar community activity, you choose to go to a community event sponsored by a Muslim mosque. The afternoon event followed a prayer activity and is primarily a bazaar that includes food booths as well as jewelry, clothing, and art artifacts. The participants include families, couples, and single people of all ages. You are surprised to see people from the South Pacific (Indonesia) as well as Chinese, East Indians, Middle Easterners, and African Americans. The lines are long at the food booths, and everyone seems to be relaxed and having a good time. Most of the women, due to their religious faith, have head coverings, including—to your surprise—the Chinese females.

### Questions for Reflection and Discussion:

1. What would you feel and think in that setting?
2. How comfortable do you imagine you would be in starting a conversation with someone? Any ideas how you might proceed with that?
3. What questions and thoughts would you come away with from such an event? What do you imagine you would gain and take away from participating in this new and unfamiliar community activity that is relevant to this population in particular or to diversity in general?

### Debriefing Questions:

1. What feelings were triggered in you as you did this exercise?
2. What was your experience in doing this?
3. What connections did you make, if any, with your life experiences?
4. What learning do you take from this activity?

*Institutional level: systemic policy and organizational practices, "business as usual,"prejudice not needed for discriminatory practices.* At the institutional level, resources and power are controlled in a systematic way that reflects dominant cultural values. These values affect individuals in ways they may be aware of, but often are not, due to the conflicted feelings that can be stirred up when exploring them. This level was discussed more fully above in the section on the Common Elements of Oppression.

The reality of disparities in many measures of the quality of life—such as health, education, income, housing, mental health, and access to services—is an indicator of this institutional level of oppression. Disparities in access to resources between the dominant, White population and diverse racial and ethnic groups are numerous and growing. The obstacles created by socioeconomic and political structures on an institutional level—such as poor housing, lack of health care, inadequate education, uneven employment, and justice systems practice—play a role that must be understood as a function of oppression on this level.

*Ideological level: societal and subcultural beliefs, values, and practices.* Ideologies are societal values and beliefs that shape thinking, particularly in relation to defining what is "good" and what "goals" one should seek. As beliefs that guide everyday activities, they are reflected in how institutions function (e.g., education, justice, family) in the dominant culture. For example, symbols that reinforce particular esthetic, behavioral qualities and norms about what is beautiful and "good" are found in all types of media. Ideologies set the criteria that are assumed to be the norm and thus play a role in illuminating what is unacceptable, inappropriate, and/or inferior (e.g., same-sex marriage, immigrant status, having a disability).

How specifically do these four levels of oppression play out in the lives of individuals? How do they combine to generate obstacles in the lives of individuals and families? Bulhan (1985) suggests that the following domains in people's lives are subject to systematic violation of basic rights in oppressive conditions:

- •*Space*: Options open to individuals and families in regard to property ownership are limited and constrained. Consider the consequences of low socioeconomic power on housing location and type. Instances of large families living together may arise more out of economic necessity than choice. What are the implications of these restrictions in terms of who owns their home versus who rents? How does home ownership or renting affect day-to-day quality of life issues?

•*Time*: Constraints imposed by responsibilities and resources shape the degree to which an individual's time is his or her own versus having to work or serve others.

•*Energy*: Activities in which one is engaged in the process of meeting one's responsibilities vary in their demands on an individual's personal resources. At issue is the degree to which an individual has control of his or her emotional, physical, and psychological energy. For example, when obtaining basic needs for food, shelter, and clothing requires one's full attention, energy must be expended at a survival level.

•*Bonding*: The development of human bonds that are essential for "good enough parenting," family and peer relationships, and intimate connections are challenging for all of us. They require substantial stable and supportive contexts as a basis to navigate through the ups and downs associated with closeness. Other issues, such as the effects of marginalization, poverty, and low social power, create obstacles that can interfere with the bonding needed for a wholesome, balanced, and active life.

•*Mobility*: How much mobility does an individual have regarding where he or she feels welcome, safe, and at home? What about the effects of segregated schools or beaches or community covenants that legally restrict who can purchase property in a given area? Can anyone with a substantive economic record such as a stable job and good salary purchase a home where he or she chooses? Take a look at places you frequent. If you were alone and in a wheelchair, how would you fare in getting around? Consider how females must take extraordinary caution about where they go, lest they be assaulted and subsequently blamed for using poor judgment. Consider gay, lesbian, bisexual, and transgender individuals who restrict their activity for fear of making themselves vulnerable.

•*Identity*: To what degree do people feel that their social identity is validated by society? Consider the constraints placed on individuals, who are targets of negative stereotypes arising from invisibility to others, and how that affects how they see themselves and their sense of validation. How does the devaluation and marginalization of an individual's group affect his or her sense of confidence and identity?

The following classroom exercise presents a case example that illustrates several of the concepts regarding oppression we have presented.

---

## Classroom Exercise 3.6 Case Vignette

Sarah and John are both African American and have been married for 9 years. They have two children, Anna, age 7, and Brian, age 4. Both grew up in multicultural, urban neighborhoods and in a working-class family where neither parent went to college, As the oldest daughter, Sarah is the one whose family always talked about her going to college. She has been working as a 5th grade teacher for the past 2 years. John, the youngest of three brothers, began working as a cashier at a computer/electronics store while in college; over the years he has moved into a middle-management position. While looking for their first home, Sarah and John encountered several obstacles, such as realtors not showing homes they had seen advertised or saying that a home was just taken off the market or went into escrow. They finally found a home that they loved for both the neighborhood, which was in close proximity to their families, and its easy access to their workplaces.

When they approached their bank about a mortgage, the bank staffer pointed out that the Federal Housing Administration and Veterans Administration had warned banks not to insure mortgages in that neighborhood. The staffer grew up in a middle-class neighborhood in the Midwest and his community life comprised primarily White ethnics, except for a few African American families who attended his family's church. To make matters worse, the disappointing news was preceded by having to wait for another bank customer who was known to the staffer and who was served before them, even though he had arrived after they did. The bank staffer noticed that the

---

Classroom Exercise 3.6 Case Vignette (continued)
familiar bank customer was in a hurry and, thinking that African Americans are unfamiliar with bank protocols and would take more time, served the late-arriving customer first.

Questions for Discussion:

1. If you were in Sarah and John's situation, how would you think and feel about difficulty in finding a home? What factors would you use to help understand their experiences?
2. Regarding the bank staffer, would you describe his behavior as prejudiced? Discriminatory? Racist? Discuss the rationale for your response.
3. What aspects of institutionalized racism/oppression are at play in this situation?
4. The bank home mortgage policy and practice were guided by concern for "maintaining" property values. Identify the pros and cons of banks refusing to insure mortgages where the neighborhood has been "redlined."
5. Given that home ownership is perhaps the most important factor in accumulating wealth that has significant implications for future generations, what are the short- and long-term consequences of these obstacles to home ownership? Consider economic, psychosocial, and community factors. What viable alternatives, if any, offer the stable base for accumulating wealth that home ownership provides?

Debriefing Questions:

1. What feelings were triggered in you as you did this exercise?
2. What was your experience in doing this?
3. What connections did you make, if any, with your life experiences?
4. What learning do you take from this activity?

# Culturally Competent Social Work

Culturally competent social work has been defined from several perspectives that are assumed to be necessary as the basis for effective practice with multicultural clients. It involves cultural awareness, knowledge acquisition, skill development, and ongoing learning from practice experience (Lum, 2003). According to the NASW (2001), cultural competence is the process by which individuals and systems respond respectfully and effectively to people of all backgrounds in ways that recognize and affirm the value of individuals, families, and communities and that refer to a set of congruent behaviors, attitudes, and policies that come together in a system, agency, and/or among professionals that enable effective practice. Cross and colleagues (1989) contribute a perspective that proposes a continuum that ranges from harm to proficiency and highlights the necessity of organizational commitment to cultural proficiency as a basis for practitioner cultural competence. Recognition is given to the combination of process (Dean, 2001) and content skills that is needed. Also, the "informed, not knowing" perspective (Anderson & Goolishian, 1992; Laird, 1998) insightfully reminds us that information about others different from ourselves attunes us to how to listen well and allow discovery with others as well as recognize our own biases.

We include a commitment to promote social justice as essential to the foundation of culturally competent practice. A clear understanding of the impact of oppressive systems on individuals, families, and communities is an essential part of such practice. Culturally competent practice occurs at all levels, so it includes work with individuals, families, organizations, and communities. It is essential to know the history and context of diverse others' experiences to assist in engaging in communication with them. It is essential that we facilitate people's telling us about their perceptions of their experience and what is important to them. Process skills used in engaging with others and initiating dialogue are quintessential cultural competency skills. The social justice perspective places particular emphasis on achieving an appreciation for diversity and oppression at institutional levels.

Social work practice that is empowerment-based, supports self-determination, and recognizes the multiple levels and dynamics of oppression and racism can in principle be called culturally competent. The following are proposed as cornerstones of such practice:

1. *Personal risk.* Willingness to put effort into learning about one's own background, history, and influences on one's life; willingness to examine how one has been affected by these factors; willingness to develop curiosity, take initiative, and "stretch" to connect with others different from oneself.

2. *Process/interaction; interpersonal skills.* Having awareness of how one affects others and willingness to adapt one's style in the interest of communicating effectively with people different from oneself. "Dynamic sizing" (Sue, 1998) involves having the skill to determine when generalizations apply versus individualizing one's perceptions to another and requires active interaction in formulating assumptions and checking them out.

3. *Content/knowledge base for developing hypotheses that are tested and modified through practice.* Effective practice with diverse others is about seeing people, families, and communities *as they see themselves.* This is particularly challenging, as individuals have a natural tendency to fit their perceptions into what is believed. After all, believing is seeing to the degree that, even in the face of information to the contrary, individuals often cling tenaciously to long-held beliefs. For example, in a new environment, tremendous detail is often missed because beliefs (such as negative or even positive stereotypes) direct one's perception.

4. *Contextual supports.* Sustained practice with diverse others that is culturally competent and proficient occurs when there is organizational identification with such efforts and validation of clients' accomplishments.

## Empowerment and Strengths-Based Practice

As noted above, culturally competent social work practice is empowerment-based (Dubois & Miley, 2005; Gutierrez, 1995; Gutierrez, DeLois, & GlenMaye, 1995; Gutierrez, Parsons & Cox, 1998; Simon, 1994; Solomon, 1976), supports self-determination, and recognizes the multiple levels and dynamics of oppression and racism. Culturally competent social workers need to be empowered to advocate for social justice themselves to be able to facilitate the empowerment of diverse clients to advocate for themselves in the face of oppressive conditions.

Traditional definitions of empowerment include phrases such as "to give power or authority to," to "authorize," "to enable or permit," "to license." This power is both internal, in terms of how efficacy is experienced, and external, in terms of the power one has to persuade others in interpersonal encounters and relationships. This power enables seeking and recognizing alternatives, particularly those related to protesting oppression and injustice at community, organizational, national, and global levels.

Empowerment is both a social and an individual process. It is social in that it occurs in a context of interaction that facilitates self-discovery. Also, it is an individual process that involves accepting personal responsibility to act and developing one's capacity to bring about change in oneself and in the environment. As power is realized, individuals become free to transform themselves and to discover untapped strengths. When individuals are empowered to advocate for social justice, authority is affirmed that already belongs to individuals as human beings and as citizens. Individual actions of protest and creativity create a ripple effect that empowers others. At the heart of the empowerment process is the phenomenon of facilitating someone to see something that he or she hasn't seen before and, subsequently, to act on that insight. It is the phenomenon of participating in others' coming to see new things as possible.

Solomon's (1976) work emphasizes the necessity of professionals being empowered as the requisite foundation for facilitating others' movement toward empowerment as well as the significant role of engaging clients through the identification of shared goals. Simon (1994) points out the fundamental value of professionals believing that individuals and environments can indeed change as a prerequisite for empowerment practice. Gutierrez, Parsons, and Cox (1998) distinguish three forms of power that underlie empowerment. *Personal* power refers to being effective in change efforts as well as being aware of the power one has, *interpersonal* power refers to an ability to influence others and developing skills to use power, and *political* power refers to influencing the allocation of resources and using varied strategies to attain those goals.

It is important to see the empowerment process as beginning with the smallest of individual actions. When joined with the actions of others, these efforts create a chain reaction that releases human energy. Over time, this energy—with a focus on social concerns—can build to a critical mass that results in social change. Each person's awareness and actions will increase the likelihood that a critical mass will develop and lead to change.

Creating a just society and world is a global issue of overwhelming proportions. A transformation from injustice and oppression to just alternatives will not come about easily or quickly. Giving birth to social justice will be a long and painful process, and it requires personal commitment and social transformation on a massive scale. Despite the magnitude of the problem, if social change for social justice is to take place, it will grow from the grass roots—at the level of individuals, small groups, local organizations, and communities. By starting at this level, the empowerment process provides a bridge connecting the person and the smaller group with larger social change movements. This bridge becomes a vehicle for change as we join with others in crossing over to yet uncharted terrain. If we trust the process, empowerment will provide the energy needed for creating a just society.

Empowerment and social movement activities and events relevant to particular groups inspire and stimulate thinking about strength-based practice at multiple levels with individuals, families, groups, communities, and organizations. Chart 3.2 illuminates some noteworthy historical factors that illustrate empowerment-based movements and actions that have been aimed at overcoming the institutionalized oppression shown in Chart 3.1.

The power of individuals acting together cannot be overestimated. As individuals engage in new and different actions, either to change their own personal situations or to change their communities, those actions can change thoughts and feelings, just as new and different thoughts can change behavior. Taking even one small step on a journey changes one's perspective on the landscape and changes one's self-definition from that of victim to that of a person with power. By taking action, commitment to effecting change is strengthened as are chances for making social change possible.

Actions become the steps on the empowerment journey, for social workers and clients alike. The first steps often are the most difficult. To act in response to social injustice involves an evolutionary process. What we are

CHART 3.2
## TIMELINE OF KEY EMPOWERMENT EVENTS AND ACTIONS IN THE UNITED STATES FOR PEOPLE OF COLOR, 1819–1962*

| | |
|---|---|
| 1827 | *Freedom's Journal*, first African American newspaper, appears |
| 1835–42 | Seminoles resist removal in Second Seminole War |
| 1859 | John Brown raids Harper's Ferry |
| 1863 | Emancipation Proclamation; African-American soldiers join Union Army |
| 1876 | Battle of Little Big Horn; Lakota and allies annihilate White troops led by Gen. Custer |
| 1880–81 | Helen Hunt Jackson's *A Century of Dishonor* influences public conscience about poor government treatment of Indians |
| 1895 | Booker T. Washington gives Atlanta Compromise speech |
| 1905 | Niagara Falls Convention promotes more militant pursuit of African American rights |
| 1909 | NAACP founded |
| 1934 | Wheeler Howard Act restores lands to tribal ownership |
| 1939 | Marian Anderson performs at Lincoln Memorial in Washington, D.C. |
| 1943 | Ban on Chinese immigration lifted |
| 1954 | *Brown v. Board of Education* rules "separate but equal" illegal |
| 1955 | Rosa Parks arrested; Montgomery bus boycott begins |
| 1956 | Congress passes Civil Rights Act; Martin Luther King Jr. founds Southern Christian Leadership Conference |
| 1960 | Sit-in Greensboro, North Carolina; Student Nonviolent Coordinating Committee formed |
| 1961 | Freedom Rides protest segregation in transportation; National Indian Youth Council formed |
| 1962 | James Meredith enters University of Mississippi |

*Adapted from Adams, Bell, & Griffin (1997, pp. 105–106).

able to do today may be radically different from what we can do next month or next year. We learn that small steps lead to larger actions in a natural progression. As first steps on the journey to cultural competence, one usually thinks more about racism and other forms of oppression and begins to talk about it with families, friends, and others in their immediate circles. Gradually, there is movement to read more about the subject, speak out at public gatherings, write letters, educate others, circulate and/or sign petitions, lobby political representatives, advocate for agency policy changes in field placements, participate in peaceful demonstrations, and organize actions with others. It is important to acknowledge all of these efforts, including the smallest ones, because social justice is accomplished by laying one brick at a time, taking one step at a time.

Actions become the impetus for growth as culturally competent social workers. The more one does, the greater the desire to know and to share what has been learned. Because actions are chosen, one can set one's own limits, and the rate of change can be controlled. To get started, all that is needed is a strong commitment to work for an end to racism and other forms of oppression and injustice. And one can learn from the examples of others. When one begins to act, actions join with the actions of others to provide the energy for the journey.

## Barriers to Empowerment

Just as it is important to understand the barriers to empowerment that clients may experience, it is essential to examine barriers that keep individuals from being advocates for social justice. A common block is a personal fear of taking risks, standing out by making a personal statement, being embarrassed in public, losing security or the respect of people who were thought to be friends, or being alienated from family.

Individuals are often deterred from social justice advocacy actions by a fear of stepping outside their personal safety zones. Everyone has spheres of operation in which there is a sense of safety. Stepping outside this area is risky because, when confronting issues in a public way, one may be subjected to the ridicule, misunderstanding, and anger of others. For example, interrupting a racist joke can be a terrifying and, thus, courageous action to take when it might evoke a negative response or prompt ostracism. The empowerment process, however, generates confidence and courage. As we become more involved with social justice actions, we discover support from others that sustains us, and we see our safety zones expand.

A significant barrier for many is the fear of creating communication gaps, tensions, and conflict within the family if prejudices within that system are identified. Applying the process of empowerment to change in the family can be helpful in this regard. There can be encouragement to be sensitive to each family member's attitude toward the issues. Unrealistic expectations about the family's response or its pace of change can create tension. Communicating consideration for others' viewpoints while respecting one's own can help reduce resistance to open discussion about the issues.

Another barrier for those who are in the dominant culture may be that of losing the privileges conferred on them based on their own social identity in an oppressive system. As one social work student wrote in his journal:

> I feel terrible about the inequities I am learning about and I want to work to change the system. I must admit, though, that I am quite ambivalent about what I might have to give up in terms of the privileges and benefits I currently get from the system as it is, since I am a White, heterosexual male. It is easy to think theoretically about social justice, but when I think in practical terms—like maybe I wouldn't get preferential treatment in a job application situation if there were truly equal opportunity—I am ashamed to say that I have to think twice.

It is important to acknowledge the courage it takes to be honest about this and to challenge oneself to face cognitive dissonance rather than slipping back into denial. Positive role models throughout history of people who were advocates for social justice can help in this regard as well.

Two additional barriers frequently impede progress in becoming social justice advocates: the fear of speaking out in public and the fear of not being sufficiently informed about the issues. By encouraging small steps, the empowerment process can be used to overcome these fears. Speaking out in public will seem less frightening if we first talk about ideas and perceptions with those with whom one feels most comfortable. Then, when individuals are ready, they can begin to speak to other people in small groups and at public meetings. It can be very rewarding to find that acquaintances and even strangers are willing to talk about racism, poverty, and oppression of other kinds. Often the message on a pin or button (e.g., "Stop Racism," "Another Student for Justice") will help begin a conversation. Speaking out is a natural outgrowth of increased commitment and involvement.

To reduce the fear of being uninformed, it is helpful to know that we can never have enough information or remember all the facts. Statistics change and one fact can counteract another. What is most important is having an understanding of underlying concepts. Once we develop a point of view as a framework for thinking, the facts will fall into place. A preponderance of information exists in books, articles, and videotapes. To make sense out of the facts, it is helpful to absorb only small amounts of information at one time and take time to process it. We are soon surprised by how much we know.

## Benefits of Empowerment

As advocates for social justice, culturally competent social workers are enriched and strengthened by the friendships they make with others who share common goals. We get to know and appreciate others whose back-grounds and lifestyles may be different from our own. People who work for social justice are old and young, rich and poor, religious and nonreligious, heterosexual and homosexual and bisexual and transsexual, and come from a variety of cultural and ethnic backgrounds. Strength grows as diversity is celebrated and differences are faced honestly. In the process we can learn to trust one another enough to live justly on a personal level.

Throughout the empowerment process, actions become seeds that ger-minate best within a supportive environment. As the seeds grow, we dis-cover that we have developed previously untapped strengths and talents. The same thing is seen happening in our clients. Taking actions they thought they could never take, when the opportunity to act presented itself, becomes liberating. Like wildflowers, actions spread, affecting others. There is a ripple effect and the circle of awareness continues to grow. As personal transformations become interwoven with social change, lives take on new meaning and deeper purpose.

The belief that actions make a difference sustains both social workers and clients in their joint efforts. Although individual acts may seem insignif-icant, they have tremendous power when joined with the efforts of count-less others. Historically, we know that social and political changes have always stemmed from the grass roots (see Chart 3.2). The abolition of slav-ery, the right to unionize, women's rights, and civil rights, to name a few—all came about as a result of grassroots efforts. If social justice is to become a reality, a collective commitment to change must be made at the local level. As more and more people unite, we gain the strength to change both the world and ourselves.

A tremendous benefit of empowerment and strengths-based practice is the satisfaction of seeing individuals and families transform their lives. As one social worker reported at a conference, "I have worked with women who were battered by their husbands for many years and have seen them come on an individual level whispering about the abuse they were enduring; later I have heard them in groups speak about their experiences without shame; and still later I have seen them organize together against violence against women. This is what empowerment-based practice is all about for me."

The next classroom exercise provides a case example for discussion regarding the social worker's cultural competence.

# Summary

In this chapter, we presented fundamental concepts and issues with the goal of providing a foundation for culturally competent social work practice. The beginning point for such a foundation is a focus on racism as the fundamental form of oppression from which other forms of oppression can be understood. Discussion about multiple identities and multiple oppressions illustrated the complex dynamics related to issues of power and privilege. Oppression is characterized by social rather than individual power, institutionalization of norms, practices, and laws that maintain their political and social hold, and are held in place by ideology and violence (real and threatened). The concept of moral exclusion was presented as a tool for helping to explore our beliefs about who is deemed worthy of being treated fairly and justly. Culturally competent social work practice is empowerment-based, supports self-determination, recognizes the multiple levels and dynamics of oppression and racism, and is grounded in and inspired by historical events and actions that have resulted in social change.

In the next chapter, we focus on racial and social identity and encourage you to think critically about your life experiences and internalization of societal beliefs as well as privilege or target status. Such reflection and processing is the basis for culturally competent social work practice.

## Classroom Exercise 3.7 Case Vignette

Kate is a 27-year-old White, ethnic female who is the youngest of three sisters and a brother. She has been in a relationship with Greg since their junior year in college. By the end of their senior year, she was beginning to feel increased pressure from him as well as from her friends to make a commitment to their relationship. Although they participated in some sexual play and even have been sexually active a few times, she primarily felt the strong tie in their relationship was based on their friendship. When he began talking about marriage, she minimized and was confused by her equally strong attraction to female friends. She didn't understand these feelings, and it was even more disconcerting that they didn't fit into any of the values or beliefs she had learned from her family or religion. Over time, the feelings of physical distance from Greg grew, and her perplexing feelings toward women not only persisted but intensified.

Kate eventually went to see a social worker to discuss her confusion and conflict. The social worker, a fundamentalist Christian, thought of homosexuality as a weakness to be fought and appealed to Kate to give up these ideas. The therapist told her, "You have the possibility of a good marriage to a man who loves you; don't lose that."

### Questions for Discussion:

1. How would you assess the social worker's cultural competence in relation to

   a) Being empowerment-based?
   b) Supporting self-determination?
   c) Recognizing the multiple levels and dynamics of oppression?

2. Based on the social worker's behavior, how would you assess her on the four cornerstones of culturally competence that were described above:

   a) Personal risk?
   b) Process/interaction; interpersonal skills?

c) Content/knowledge base for developing hypotheses that are tested and modified through practice?

d) Contextual supports?

3. To better understand Kate's situation, what does the social worker need to learn about gay and lesbian social movements and social justice activities? How would a historical understanding help the social worker understand Kate's journey toward empowerment?

*Debriefing Questions:*

1. What feelings were triggered in you as you did this exercise?

2. What was your experience in doing this?

3. What connections did you make, if any, with your life experiences?

4. What learning do you take from this activity?

# References

Adams, M., Bell, L., & Griffin, P. (Eds.). (1997). *Teaching for diversity and social justice.* App. 5B. New York: Routledge.

Allport, G. (1954). *The nature of prejudice.* Reading, MA: Addison-Wesley.

Anderson, H., & Goolishian, H. A. (1992). The client is the expert: A not-knowing approach to therapy. In S. McNamee & K. Gergen (Eds.). *Therapy as social construction* (pp. 25–39). Newbury Park, CA: Sage Publications.

Blumenfeld, W. J., & Raymond, D. (2000). Prejudice and discrimination. In M. Adams, W. J. Blumenfeld, R. Castenada, H. W. Hackman, M. L. Peters, & X. Zuniga (Eds.), *Readings for diversity and social justice* (pp. 21–30). New York: Routledge.

Bulhan, H. A. (1985). *Frantz Fanon and the psychology of oppression.* New York: Plenum Press.

Cross, T., Bazron, B., Dennis, K., & Isaacs, M. (1989). *Towards a culturally competent system of care.* Vol. 1. Washington, DC: CASSP Technical Assistance Center, Georgetown University Child Development Center.

Dean, R. (2001). The myth of cross-cultural competence. *Families in Society: The Journal of Contemporary Human Services, 82*(6), 623–630.

DeRosa, P. (1988). *The four ism's.* Unpublished manuscript. Available at ChangeWorks Consulting, 28 S. Main Street #113, Randolph, MA 02368, (781) 986-6150, www.changeworksconsulting.org.

Deutsch, M. (1990). Psychological roots of moral exclusion. *Journal of Social Issues, 46*(1), 21–26.

Dubois, B. & Miley, K. (2005). *Social work: An empowering profession.* Boston: Allyn and Bacon/Longman.

Gaertner, S. L., & Dovidio, J. F. (1981). Racism among the well-intentioned. In E. Clausen & J. Bermingham (Eds.), *Pluralism, racism and public policy: The search for equality* (pp. 145–159). New York: Macmillan.

Garcia-Bahne, B. (1981). *Ideological images: Social psychological considerations on the stereotyping process.* Paper presented at the Conference on Ethnic American Women, Program for the Study of Women and Men in Society, University of Southern California, Los Angeles.

Gil, D. (1998). *Confronting injustice and oppression.* New York: Columbia University Press.

Giroux, H. A. (2000). Racial politics, pedagogy, and the crisis of representation in academic multiculturalism. *Social Identities, 6*(4), 493–510.

Goldberg, D. T. (1993). *Racist culture.* Cambridge, MA: Basil Blackwell.

Gutierrez, L. M. (1995). Understanding the empowerment process: Does consciousness make a difference? *Social Work Research, 19*(4), 229–237.

Gutierrez, L. M., DeLois, K. A., & GlenMaye, L. (1995). Understanding empowerment practice: Building on practitioner-based knowledge. *Families in Society, 76*(8), 534–542.

Gutierrez, L., Parsons, R. J., & Cox, E. J. (1998). *Empowerment in social work practice.* Pacific Grove, CA: Brooks/Cole.

Kovel (1984). *White racism.* New York: Columbia University Press.

Laird, J. (1998). Theorizing culture. In M. McGoldrick (Ed.), *Re-Visioning family therapy* (pp. 20–36). New York: The Guilford Press.

Lichtenberg, P., van Beusekom, J., & Gibbons, D. (1997). *Encountering bigotry:*

*Befriending projecting persons in everyday life.* Northvale, NJ: Jason Aronson Inc.

Lott, B. (2002). Cognitive and behavioral distancing from the poor. *American Psychologist, 57*(2), 100–110.

Lum, D. (2003). *Culturally competent practice: A framework for growth and action* (2nd ed.). New York: Thomson Brooks/Cole.

McIntosh, P. (1989, July/August). Unpacking the invisible knapsack: White privilege. *Peace and Freedom,* pp. 10–12.

NASW. (2001). *NASW standards for cultural competence in social work practice.* Washington, DC: Author.

Opotow, S. (1990). Moral exclusion and injustice: An introduction. *Journal of Social Issues, 46*(1), 1–20.

Omni, M., & Winant, H. (1986). *Racial formation in the United States.* New York: Routledge & Kegan Paul.

Pharr, S. (1988). *Homophobia: A weapon of sexism.* Inverness, CA: Chardon Press.

Pincus, F.L. (2000). Discrimination comes in man forms: Individual, institutional and structural. In M. Adams, W. J. Blumenfeld, R. Castenada, H. W. Hackman, M. L. Peters, & X. Zuniga (Eds.), *Readings for diversity and social justice* (pp. 31–35). New York: Routledge.

Pinderhughes, E. (1989). *Understanding race, ethnicity, and power.* New York: Free Press.

Rose, S. (2002, March). *Social work at the crossroads—A reflection.* Paper presented at the Social Work at the Crossroads Conference, California State University, Fresno, Department of Social Work Education.

Simon, B. (1994). *The empowerment tradition in American social work.* New York: Columbia University Press.

Solomon, B. (1976). *Black empowerment.* New York: Columbia University Press.

Sue, S. (1998). In search of cultural competence in psychotherapy and counseling. *American Psychologist, 53*(4), 440–448.

Tatem, B. D. (2000). Defining racism: "Can we talk?" In M. Adams, W. J. Blumenfeld, R. Castenada, H. W. Hackman, M. L. Peters, & X. Zuniga (Eds.), *Readings for diversity and social justice* (pp. 79–82). New York: Routledge.

Wildman, S. M., & Davis, A. D. (2000). Language and silence: Making systems of privilege visible. In M. Adams, W. J. Blumenfeld, R. Castenada, H. W. Hackman, M. L. Peters, & X. Zuniga (Eds.), *Readings for diversity and social justice* (pp. 50–60). New York: Routledge.

Young, I. M. (2000). Five faces of oppression. In M. Adams, W. J. Blumenfeld, R. Castenada, H. W. Hackman, M. L. Peters, & X. Zuniga (Eds.), *Readings for diversity and social justice* (pp. 35–49). New York: Routledge.

# Chapter Four
# Social and Racial Identity

Identity develops through life experiences that promote an integrated sense of self. This sense of self embodies the beliefs, values, interests, and hopes that provide a basis for connections with others and point to future life directions. Developmental psychosocial theory identifies normative psychological and social tasks that confront all of us in the process of developing, among other things, self-confidence, connections with others, intimate relationships, complexity of thinking, meaningful life work, and ultimately successful aging.

In this chapter, we deal specifically with the concept of social identity as related to ethnicity and what is called "race." Social and racial identity complements and is inextricably connected to understanding and making a commitment to social justice, the focus of chapter 1. The stance in this book is that cultural competency requires the integration of diversity and social justice. In this chapter we focus on understanding one's own social and racial identity as an essential component of cultural competence.

In chapter 2 we set forth our view of race as a social construct that is relational and political and the belief that the development of cultural competence begins with understanding racism as the fundamental oppressive system in the United States. This approach expands cultural competent practice to include knowledge of all forms of oppression. Racial identity development models address the process of coming to terms with our identity based on race within the context of a racist society. Similarly, social identity development processes address coming to terms with our identities based on membership in other groups. The concept of social identity is integral to understanding oppression in that oppression is experienced on the basis of stereotyped characteristics that ascribe low or high social power (e.g., race, ethnicity, gender, sexual orientation, physical ability, socioeconomic class, age, religion) to groups with which one identifies. These identities are fundamental elements of our self-concept, and their combination in different configurations can have a powerful influence on how we understand our life experiences (Robinson & Howard-Hamilton, 2000).

The following reflection exercise provides an opportunity for you to think about your own experiences related to your ethnicity and how others' expectations have influenced your identity.

---

**REFLECTION EXERCISE 4.1  ETHNICITY AND EXPECTATIONS**

Think about your answers to the following questions. It may be helpful to write your responses so you can refer to them later and/or consider sharing some of them with others in class.

1. When did you first become aware of your ethnicity as White, African American, Latino/a, Asian, Native American, or other ethnicity? What was that experience? What positive or negative associations do you have with that memory?

2. What memories do you have about learning about others' differences?

3. When you look back on beginning to talk about sensitive issues around difference, what do you think made it so difficult to talk about diversity and difference? For yourself? For others?

4. What expectations do you recall that you felt related to you based on your social identity? How was the group you identified with "supposed" to "be" or to "act?"

---

We focus in this chapter on how social power and socioeconomic class affect how you experience your ethnicity and on processes that prompt change in your life experience. Your making connections regarding how your ethnic/racial identity is influenced by the sociopolitical context in which you grew up and the formative dominant society values embodied in that environment is a fundamental part of awareness building. Racial and ethnic identity concepts draw attention to the central role that social power (vis-à-vis oppression, privilege, and socioeconomic class) has in shaping identity. By understanding the concepts, it is hoped you will be encouraged to explore your relationship, as it evolves over time, with the values and identifications of the dominant societal ideology (i.e., the "shoulds" and values related to what is considered normative and "good"). As you read about some of the experiences of social work student Caterina below, notice the change process in which she is engaged related to her identity.

> Caterina is a Latina student living in a new city in the Southwest. She is working on her master's degree in social work. Through curriculum and field education experiences, she is exposed to learning about diversity. As part of her education she has the opportunity to observe community people engaged in advocacy efforts. Much of what she witnesses in community and town hall meetings involves citizen complaints about city or county practices. Experiencing the passion of community people from all walks of life and socioeconomic classes as they express concerns and hold public officials accountable is new to her. One night she is particularly impressed when White, upper-middle-class citizens, some of them professors from the university, participate in a meeting about an incident in which an African American school principal was unfairly stopped in traffic and required to lie spread-eagle on the street while police checked her documents. The next day, as Caterina is shopping for a new sweater in the upscale mall that she enjoys going to occasionally, she notices—for the first time and in a different way—that the few Latinos there, apart from herself, are menial workers. All the shoppers are White and most are middle and upper class. She feels like a door of new awareness is opening for her.

Caterina's experiences provide an introduction to several important concepts about racial and social identity that are discussed in this chapter. As her account demonstrates, we respond, as meaning-making beings, to others based on meanings we attach to their behavior (Berger & Luckman, 1966). As you consider the vignette, keep in perspective assumptions that you bring about Latinos regarding homogeneity and heterogeneity with that population and about acculturation. We tend to create a sense of self that, in part, is based on what significant others expect of us. The sociopolitical context in which this process occurs is enormously instrumental in shaping the direction in which identity develops. Caterina's experiences illustrate that all individuals internalize oppression and racism merely by virtue of exposure to socialization in an oppressive and racist environment. Exposure to socialization isn't good or bad; we don't choose to be exposed to it. However, what is important is what we choose to do with our learning about that socialization. Again, as Caterina's story shows, exposure to new experiences and socialization processes provides the foundation for developing a socially conscious self. The personal work in which she is engaged through her social work education complements the social advocacy work she is observing at the organizational and institutional levels. Her learning process involves changing how she views society, how she views herself, and how she sees herself as an agent of change. It is an emotional and intellectual change process that engages her in reflecting on how oppression has influenced her life and her relationships. The process is complex and involves making connections between social, political, and institutional factors and her personal experience.

In this chapter, we first discuss the dynamics and tasks you can expect to experience as you explore and learn about your social and racial identity. We then present aspects of social identity related to ethnicity, an important concept for understanding the role of oppression, racism, and social power in the formation of identity. After focusing on social identity in general, we discuss social identity in relation to oppression and present three models of racial identity development.

# The Learning Process: Exploring Your Social and Racial Identity

Social and racial identity involves developmental dynamics associated with the process of recognizing racism and oppression in your social environment and in yourself. The racial identity models presented later in this chapter highlight the tasks involved in this developmental process. Many of us have characteristics related to *both* the experience of having privilege and the experience of being targets of oppression. This means that the work of becoming aware of your social and racial identity often involves dealing with conflicts, tensions, or anxieties related to coming to terms with what these experiences mean in your life.

Social and racial identity models provide a lens, so to speak, with which to examine and appreciate all of the different aspects of identity associated with different sociocultural backgrounds, family, and national origins. While we usually experience the psychological and social processes as deeply personal, they are powerfully influenced by dominant societal ideologies. This presents tremendous challenges that must be dealt with in the process of developing a wholesome, integrated sense of self where confidence is premised on a personal, freely chosen definition of self.

Social and racial identity development processes involve engagement in *affective learning*. Your task is to engage in cognitive learning about oppression and your own beliefs. An equally important task is to examine your feelings about those beliefs and to process those feelings. This means recognizing your feelings, naming them, processing the meanings they hold for you, and making changes in accordance with how you see or want to see yourself. Through engaging in these processes, you develop insight into factors that contribute to the expectations others hold and how you view those expectations. By dealing with your feelings about difference and diversity, you will be able to make connections among life events, societal and institutional factors, and your personal experiences. This leads to feeling less vulnerable and intimidated in the face of powerful reactions of others to sensitive topics related to racism. As a result of doing the work, you can gain a new perspective that helps address fears or anxieties about being called pejorative, hateful terms associated with your social identity based on either your having race privilege or being a target of negative stereotypes based on your race.

As you engage in exploring your own social and racial identity and addressing issues related to diversity and social justice, we suggest that you keep a journal of your process as suggested in the following reflection exercise.

**REFLECTION EXERCISE 4.2  JOURNALING AND AFFECTIVE LEARNING**

Consider keeping a journal for this class that includes the following:

1. Identify and list the thoughts and feelings on a weekly basis that are triggered for you as you sit in on class lectures, watch videos, engage in readings, and observe and/or participate in class discussion.

2. Transform those thoughts and feelings into a statement you would make to someone else about your perspective on that point, theme, or observation, for example, "I think . . ." "When I heard x, y, z, I thought and felt . . ." "When I heard x say yz, I questioned whether. . ."

3. Identify whom you would feel safe communicating those statements to and whom you would not. Say something about why these people might feel safe or unsafe.

# Key Identity Development Concept: What Does Ethnicity Mean?

It is important to understand the concept of ethnicity as it contributes to what we are calling social identity. Phinney (1996) describes three dynamics related to ethnicity that apply to all groups, regardless of national origin (e.g., Euro-American or ethnic "minority"). They are discussed briefly below.

1. *Cultural values, attitudes, and behaviors that distinguish groups.* An aspect of a person's ethnicity is related to the cultural identifications he or she holds. A person's thoughts, feelings, and behaviors are related to these values in such a way that they can reflect traditional and/or dominant culture perspectives (e.g., family and/or individualistic, competitive and/or collective values). A person can hold *both* sets of

values in differing intensities. The complexity and richness of a culture is lost through stereotyping processes that lead to generalizations. For example, outsiders might expect all Southeast Asians to be Buddhist or Taoist, when in fact some are Christian or followers of Shamanism.

2. *Subjective sense of ethnic group membership; strength, salience, and meaning of ethnic identity.* This dynamic is related to the degree to which a person identifies with his or her cultural identifications and how prominent they are in the person's life. Little can be assumed about someone's ethnic identity without inquiry in this regard. Ethnic identity can be strong even without involvement in cultural activities (Keefe, 1992; Keefe & Padilla, 1987), can change dramatically within the first generation due to acculturation, or can reflect multiple identifications (e.g., Italian and Armenian, Black and Jewish, Chinese and Muslim). Culture is fluid, not static, in that it represents adaptation. Cultural aspects with which someone identifies are truly unique to that person, and any assumptions premised on someone's phenotype, language, or ethnicity are truly misguided until one speaks with that person. Intergenerational conflict between immigrant parents and American-born children is legend due to the vast adaptations that the younger generation makes in the new setting, especially through media exposure to the new culture.

3. *Experiences associated with diversity status, including powerlessness, discrimination, and prejudice.* When a person feels marginalized, invisible to others, or devalued due to low social power, this can have powerful consequences on what that person identifies with and how.

The three aspects outlined above suggest that ethnicity is not something that can be dealt with by pigeonholing someone; it needs to be viewed as varying "along a number of dimensions" (Phinney, 1996, p. 924). We propose that formative factors in creating that variation along the three dimensions include socioeconomic class, phenotype, gender, physical and mental ability, sexual orientation, age, length of residence in the United States, immigration status, religious orientation, and developmental concerns related to social identity and racial identity development. The next reflection exercise provides an opportunity for you to explore your ethnicity and its significance for you.

REFLECTION EXERCISE 4.3  **EXPLORING YOUR ETHNIC IDENTITY**

1. Describe your family and national origins. What are they? Identify as many as you are aware of.

2. How do you identify with them? Do you find them all mutually important, or do you see one or some as more significant than others?

3. What supports or obstacles/lack of supports were present in your family or among friends in learning about your own social identity?

4. What activities did you engage in, or would desire to engage in, in relation to your social identity in the past or present?

# Social Identity

Social identity refers to at least two dynamics, both of which are influenced by social power, that have a role in identity formation. First, there is what some have called an aspect of "communality" that individuals feel with others.[1] Communality occurs through cultural identification and reference groups that speak to one's interests. The second dynamic, labeled social power, is an aspect of identity that is affected by oppression regardless of whether one is a beneficiary of privilege or a target of oppression.

To better understand the potent role of social power, we review two approaches to the development of social identity. The first examines three different domains—related to what we are born with, what resources are developed in our lifetime, and the sociopolitical context into which we are born—that combine to shape our unique and individual social identity. The

---

1. Social identity deals with "communality" in that it deals with reference groups with which individuals identify. Racial identity specifically deals with the process of recognizing the internalization of racism, the tasks of undoing the internalization, and developing a racist-free identity. The latter is discussed in more detail in the next section.

second approach identifies processes individuals go through in coming to terms with oppression and racism in society. Both of these two distinct approaches illuminate the significance of sociopolitical dynamics in personal life and combine to clarify the differences in people's lives that lead some to recognize and confront oppression sooner than others.

# Three Dimensions of Social Identity

Arredondo and colleagues (1996) suggest that three distinct dimensions of life experiences combine and interact in the process of forming one's social identity. They are summarized in Table 4.1.

The *"A" dimension* represents characteristics into which you are born and over which you have the least control. These characteristics are much more susceptible to negative stereotypes than the other two dimensions. On a continuum, all of the factors listed in the "A" dimension in the table below are the basis of either oppression or privilege. Characteristics such as culture are often more vulnerable to stereotyping depending on language, accent, dress, practices, and political climate. For example, anti-immigrant sentiments affect immigrants from Western Europe as well as those from other parts of the world. Your social status is affected by virtue of your being young or elderly, being identified as dominant culture or as ethnic minority culture, being male or female, being predominantly English-speaking or speaking another language, being a person with a disability or not, being heterosexual or homosexual, and, perhaps most significantly having low or high income status. While these characteristics are presented in an "either/or" perspective, in reality they are not necessarily mutually exclusive as categories. For example, sexuality and gender identity are not precisely grasped in either/or male or female terms, but are perhaps better described as being on a continuum, where individual preferences for connections with others (i.e., friendships, intimacy) and self-presentation (e.g., attire) are described more accurately as being "more of one gender" than the other.

Your experiences with the characteristics in the "A" dimension affect how comfortable you may be in honoring *all* of the heritage and traditions that combine to create your cultural identification. When the lack of validation for some facet of your personal history results in your own minimizing

## TABLE 4.1  DIMENSIONS OF SOCIAL IDENTITY

**"A" Dimension: What we are born with**
- Age/developmental issues
- Culture
- Ethnicity
- Gender
- Language
- Disability
- Sexual orientation
- Socioeconomic class (i.e., income, education)

**"B" Dimension: Resources we develop**
- Level of education (e.g., more women going into higher education since advent of the women's movement)
- Geographic location; regional culture
- Income level
- Relationship status (i.e. married, divorced, single)
- Religion/spirituality beliefs
- Work experience; having a "career" versus a "job"
- Citizenship status; nondocumentation, citizenship
- Military experience
- Recreational interests

**"C" Dimension: Sociopolitical context**
- Historical, political, sociocultural, and economic contexts
    - Values associated with your generation (e.g., the '30s generation (Depression era), the '60s (e.g., music, antiwar, social movements, lifestyle options)
    - Psychosocial effects of liberal or conservative political values
    - Privileges or limitations related to your access to socioeconomic resources
- Sociopolitical, global, and environmental events of a form that affect your personal culture and life experiences; these factors can affect how you are treated and perceived For example:
    - How events such as the war in Iraq influence everyday life in the United States and traveling abroad for Americans
    - How current sociopolitical events and the growth of religious fundamentalism shape how many Americans think about diversity, about cultural and religious "difference"

of aspects of your background, this creates hurdles that need to be over-come in the process of developing a wholesome identity.

The *"B" dimension*, the resources you develop for yourself in your life-time, is seen as resulting from the interactions between what you are born with ("A") and the sociopolitical context of your life ("C"). For example, how you fare as a female in a career is influenced to a large degree by the sociopolitical climate, such as the presence of a powerful social movement like feminism. Likewise, a person with a disability has far more resources at hand since the passage of the Americans with Disabilities Act than before its ratification. The Vietnam War had dire consequences for someone in the National Guard and males of eligible age when the military draft was in place. The opportunity to pursue a career with increased responsibility and salary is dependent on privileges related to socioeconomic class that enable access to higher education; when such privilege is not present, employment most often is viewed as a "job" that provides a certain hourly wage.

The *"C" dimension*, the sociopolitical context of your life, is often diffi-cult to recognize until you are out of that context. Sometimes it is through looking back on your experiences that you can see patterns more clearly between factors in the sociopolitical context and your perspectives and life decisions. Various historical contexts and events—from war and devastation (e.g., Vietnam War, 9/11, Iraq) to social values (e.g., social movements of the 1960s; cultural value on materialism, individualism, and consumerism)—influence different generations' hope or loss of hope for a future. The late 20th- and early 21st-century contexts have resulted in increased concerns among younger generations about the prospect of a nuclear holocaust, loss of employment opportunities, threatened loss of socially subsidized retire-ment program, health insurance, and lessened prospects for buying a home.

For those who experience oppression and racism, the "A" dimension is the most powerful. This is illustrated by a few examples. If you are poor and African American, Latino/a, or White ethnic, you encounter greater struggles in accessing sound education, careers, health services, and housing of your choice. Evidence shows that 1 of 10 African American males is at risk for incarceration, and more African American males have been involved in justice systems than have attended college. Latinos/as continue to have low high school completion rates, Latinas are entering the prison system in increasing numbers, and, as a whole, the Latino/a population is at risk for early death and impaired health due to serious but treatable health disorders, such as diabetes. The poverty and suicide rates for Native Americans continue to be high compared with all other population groups. In times of war we are reminded that, for many low-income ethnic minorities, military service is the only viable means for achieving stable employment and securing higher education and/or training in skills that will make them competitive in the job market. The following exercise asks you to reflect on your social identity by using the three dimensions of your life experiences.

## REFLECTION EXERCISE 4.4   SOCIAL IDENTITY DIMENSIONS

1. List all of the characteristics with which you were born ("A" dimension). Which of these characteristics result in benefits of privilege for you? Which of them result in negative stereotypes and result in your being a target of oppression?

2. List the resources that you have developed for yourself up to this point in your life and make a separate list of the resources you seek in the future ("B" dimension). If you don't have an image of the future, say that, too.
   •Next to each item on your list of hopes and intentions, identify factors (parents, family, teachers, media, friends) that have had a role in shaping those hopes and intentions.

3. Make a list of the different events in the sociopolitical context of your life so far ("C" dimension). What are you aware of in your immediate or more remote environment that influences how you see yourself, your present options, and your future? Respond to any of the factors identified in Table 4.1 for the "C" dimension and/or identify others that might not be described there.

4. Reflect on how the interactions between the characteristics with which you were born ("A") and the sociopolitical context in which you live ("C") have influenced the resources you have developed for yourself and your hopes for the future ("B").

# Racial Identity and Oppression

Jackson and Hardiman (n.d.) propose that all of us, regardless of background, engage in similar processes as we struggle with the meaning of oppression. At an initial stage, we are naïvely blind to oppression in society and in ourselves. This naïveté is jarred when we recognize that our worldview does not explain our observations of injustice or does not provide a basis of healthy self-acceptance. Similarly, at other points, individuals may realize a contradiction between their views and life experiences. This triggers further movement toward the goal of increased social consciousness. Once people are aware of oppression, they can move to *accepting* it, either *actively* or *passively*. The distinction between active and passive acceptance is related to how aware we are of our identification with oppression, either as a beneficiary or a target, and acknowledgment of its patterns in society. This stage is followed by *resistance* to oppression, again either *active* or *passive*. Active resistance involves open questioning, developing insight into painful feelings about oppression (e.g., anger, pain, hurt, and rage), beginning to recognize the role of power and an ability to affect our environment, and understanding more about who we are. Passive resistance does not involve risk taking, but it does involve experiences of frustration, pain, and anger that potentially provoke greater risk taking and, slowly but surely, a motivation to know more about who we are. A third stage, *redefinition*, leads to exploration of self-definition, connecting with relevant reference groups, "naming" ourselves as belonging to a group, and feeling increased understanding of ourselves. The final point, *internalization,* is characterized by an infusion of a new self-understanding into other parts of our life, stronger feelings about the new identity, and actions that are in line with maintaining the new consciousness (e.g., learning, participating in new activities, changing our social network).

Helms (1990) defines racial identity and racial identity development theory as "a sense of group or collective identity based on one's perception that he or she shares a common racial heritage with a particular racial group . . . racial identity development theory concerns the psychological implications of racial-group membership, that is, belief systems that evolve in reaction to perceived differential racial-group membership" (p. 3). Everyone, regardless of background, will deal with racial identity in some form.

Racial identity development models address the change process that we go through as we work through and reject oppression throughout our lifetime. Given the dominant/subordinate, privileged/oppressed relationship of Euro-Americans and people of color in society, it is not surprising that the developmental change process unfolds in different ways. Before reading about the three racial identity models that follow, we suggest that you engage in the following classroom exercise, which seeks to stimulate your awareness of how you either benefit from or are disadvantaged by your membership in a group based on race, and to illustrate how perceptions differ based on group membership and the racial identity development state that you are currently in.

---

## Classroom Exercise 4.1 The Visit*

Consider the following parable. Suspend disbelief and assume that what follows might actually happen. If you are White, read the first paragraph. If you are a person of color, read the second paragraph. If you are biracial or multiracial, you may either choose which paragraph to read or read both.

Paragraph One:
"You will be visited tonight by an official you have never met. He will begin by telling you that he is extremely embarrassed. The organization he represents has made a mistake, something that hardly ever happens. According to its records, he goes on, you were to have been born Black: to another set of parents, far from where you were raised. However, the rules being what they are, this error must be rectified and as soon as possible. So at midnight tonight, you will become Black. And this will mean not simply a darker skin, but the bodily and facial features associated with African ancestry. However, inside, you will be the person you have always been. Your knowledge and ideas will remain intact, but, outwardly, you will not be recognizable to anyone you now know. Your visitor emphasizes that being born to the wrong parents was in no way your fault. Consequently, his organization is prepared to offer you some reasonable compensation. Would you, he asks, care to name a sum of money you might consider appropriate? He adds that his group is by no means poor. It can be quite generous when the circum-

stances warrant, as they seem to in your case. He finishes by saying that the group's records show you that are scheduled to live another 50 years as a Black man or woman in America. *How much financial compensation would you request and why?"*

Paragraph Two:
You will be visited tonight by an official you have never met. He will begin by telling you that he is extremely embarrassed. The organization he represents has made a mistake, something that hardly ever happens. According to its records, he goes on, you were to have been born White: to another set of parents, far from where you were raised. However, the rules being what they are, this error must be rectified and as soon as possible. So at midnight tonight, you will become White. And this will mean not simply having White skin, but the bodily and facial features associated with European ancestry. However, inside, you will be the person you have always been. Your knowledge and ideas will remain intact, but, outwardly, you will not be recognizable to anyone you now know. Your visitor emphasizes that being born to the wrong parents was in no way your fault. Consequently, his organization is prepared to offer you some reasonable compensation. Would you, he asks, care to name a sum of money you might consider appropriate? He adds that his group is by no means poor. It can be quite generous when the circumstances warrant, as they seem to in your case. He finishes by saying that the group's records show that you are scheduled to live another 50 years as a White man or woman in America. *How much financial compensation would you request and why?"*

Discussion:
In small groups, answer the question posed at the end of each paragraph: *How much money would you request?* Keep a record of what points or factors you considered in your deliberations.

How did the responses of members of your group differ?

Discuss how different members of your group calculated the value they placed on their own skin color. What meanings do you ascribe to the calculations?

---

* Adapted from Hacker (1992, pp. 31–32).

In the next three sections, we present racial identity development models for African Americans, ethnic Whites, and multicultural individuals. While there is no model related specifically to other people of color (e.g., Latinos/as, Asian Pacific Islanders, Native Americans), there is evidence to suggest that the process for other people of color is similar to that described for African Americans (Highlen et al., 1988; Phinney, 1990). The assumption is that most people of color must deal with the task of recognizing the internalization of racism and undoing its effects. This perspective supports the view that no one remains untouched by dominant, mainstream society's devaluation of "minority status." All people of color must deal with the reality of discrimination and racism, and their effects on their lives, just as people of privileged backgrounds must deal with its effects.

The three models include tasks involved in personally confronting racism and undoing its effects on your identity. In all models, it is assumed that a positive sense of yourself as a member of your group is important for psychological health. The models highlight the tasks involved in confronting your experiences as either privileged and/or oppressed. This can mean dealing with multiple identities that embody both privilege and target status. For example, those with both a European and a Hispanic heritage must deal with the meaning of both of these for themselves. The models identify various points of awareness on a proposed continuum of development that affect your perception and experience.

The models address the internalization of dominant ideological belief systems, realization of an identity based on privilege or marginalization, and movement toward the formulation of an identity that no longer needs a self-definition that is contingent on the "other." According to the models, when you have a wholesome identity, you have the capacity to own characteristics that had been projected onto others in the form of negative stereotypes. You are free of the distortion that comes from privileged or targeted status. The distortions to be undone for those in a dominant position involve undoing the overestimations of self that come from a status of privilege and entitlement. The distortions to be undone for those in a subordinate position involve undoing the underestimations of self and giving up the devaluation of their group that was projected on them by dominant ideology and internalized by them as members of the devalued group.

The racial identity development models propose that you move through a series of points or statuses, and that you transition from one point to another on a continuum of development through successive statuses that represent attitudinal (i.e., behavior, affect, cognition) processes that regulate how you interpret racial information (Helms, 1995). Helms suggests that movement from one status to another is influenced by how people cope, that is, what information processing strategies you use. The models propose that change is triggered when existing perceptions are too limited to help you cope with a personally meaningful racial event. Coping responses are seen as varying among different racial groups based on the effects of social categorization and dissimilarities in social power. While the processes are presented in linear form, in fact it is probably more accurate to think of the stages in spiral form. You may move from one stage to the next, only to revisit an earlier stage as the result of new experiences.

Racial identity development models offer frameworks for understanding personal change that begin with lack of awareness of dominant societal oppression and move toward development of an integrated wholesome identity. This identity is free of being defined in relation to the "other"; in other words, an identity that is defined on its own terms rather than being defined by a context imbued with a biased distribution of power and privilege. While there is still little empirical work on these models, they do provide provocative paradigms for grappling with the psychological consequences of social ideology and for thinking critically about diversity within a social justice framework.

## Black Racial Identity Development

As a social construct, race fulfills economic and social functions and plays a formative role in one's psychosocial development. Earlier, in chapter 2, we emphasized race as a social construct that is a relational and political concept. Black racial identity models bring to light the consequences of racism on a person's awareness related to his or her identification as being Black. The Cross (1995) Black Identity Development Model identifies movement through points that at one end of the continuum represent internalization of negative stereotypes and devaluation of oneself and one's group. At the opposite end of the continuum is self-confidence based on internalization of a new racist-free identity. It is proposed that the change process is initiated either by an event that devastates one's identity or worldview or by a "series of smaller, eye-opening episodes" that elicit anger and guilt. These events lead to less engagement with dominant society and more immersion into one's own group, followed by the development of an identity that meets new personal needs (Cross, 1995, p. 105).

The model outlines personal and social change through passages conceptualized as "ego statuses" that included preencounter, encounter, immersion/emersion, internalization, and internalization/commitment. Racial identity development involves a renunciation of internalized racism and the emergence of a positive racial identity as a Black person.

- *Preencounter* consciousness and behavior is characterized by an out-of-awareness devaluation of oneself and one's group, along with efforts to "fit into" dominant cultural life. In this stage, the person has absorbed many of the beliefs and values of the dominant White culture, including the notion that "White is right" and "Black is wrong." While internalization of Black stereotypes may be outside conscious awareness, the person seeks to assimilate and be accepted by Whites and actively or passively distances himself or herself from other Blacks. This deemphasis on his or her racial-group membership may allow the person to think that race has not been or will not be a relevant factor in his or her own achievement and may contribute to a belief in a U.S. meritocracy that is often a part of the preencounter worldview.

- The *encounter* stage is a two-part process that involves the person experiencing an event that challenges his or her current worldview and precipitates an interpretation of the event from a new perspective. Sue and Sue (2003) suggest that an event, such as the death of Martin Luther King Jr., can stimulate a shift in worldview because one's prior worldview cannot explain his death. On a personal level, instances of social rejection by White friends or colleagues may lead the person to conclude that many Whites will not view him or her as an equal. Faced with the reality that he or she cannot truly be White, the person is compelled to focus on his or her identity as a member of a group targeted by racism. Such a shift can be accompanied by feelings of anger and guilt as the person is forced to acknowledge the impact of racism on his or her life.

- The *immersion/emersion* stage is characterized by a focus of a person's full attention on his or her own culture. An increasing sense of cultural pride develops. This stage is characterized by the simultaneous desire to be surrounded with visible symbols of the person's racial identity and active avoidance of symbols of Whiteness. As the person transitions through this stage, anger may be experienced against Whites. This anger typically dissipates as much of the person's energy is directed toward his or her own group and self-exploration. The result of this exploration is an emerging security in a newly defined and affirmed sense of self.

- In the *internalization* stage, the person is secure in his or her own sense of racial identity. Pro-Black attitudes in general become more expansive, open, and less defensive. While still maintaining his or her connections with Black peers, the internalized person is willing to establish meaningful relationships with Whites who acknowledge and are respectful of his or her self-definition. The person is also ready to build coalitions with members of other oppressed groups.

- The final stage, *internalization/commitment*, is psychologically similar to the internalization stage. However, the person at this stage has found ways to translate his or her personal sense of being Black into action or commitment to the concerns of Black people as a group. With a positive sense of racial identity, the person is able to perceive proactively and transcend race. This new racist-free identity is one that meets his or her new personal needs and is reflected in a commitment over time to Black community concerns (Cross, 1995).

If you are Black or a person of color from another racial/ethnic group, the next exercise is aimed at promoting your discovery or rediscovery of your feelings about your race.

# White Racial Identity Development

White racial identity development models point to racism as a significant aspect of being a White ethnic. They highlight how Whites are socialized into perceiving themselves as being entitled to privilege and into maintaining their privileged status through mechanisms such as denial, distortion, and aggression (Hardiman, 1982; Helms, 1999). The models also illuminate how movement through the development continuum points or statuses

**REFLECTION EXERCISE 4.5**
**REDISCOVERING MY FEELINGS ABOUT BEING A PERSON OF COLOR\***

Think back to when you first became truly aware that you were a person of color. Close your eyes and imagine yourself back in the situation. Try to feel what you felt at the time. Focus on *yourself* rather than on other people. Write about your experience in your journal.

1. Who was involved in the situation, and what were their races?

2. What happened to you?

3. When that happened, you felt . . .

4. Describe your bodily sensations at the time.

5. What did you do in response to your feelings or bodily sensations?

6. How did you feel about being a person of color when this particular situation was over?

7. What did you learn about being (your race)?

You may want to try this exercise several times, using experiences from different times in your life for analysis.

Refer back to your analyses of yourself. We hope they provided some ideas about how you react daily to being a person of color. Review the stages of Black racial identity development presented previously and think about where you might be in your own development. Consider keeping a daily diary in which you record your experiences of consciously being a person of color.

————
\*Adapted from Helms (1992, pp. 69–72).

involves recognition of how, by exercising privilege, a person has participated in oppressive practices. The person moves to confronting his or her biases and prejudices and, ultimately, to taking responsibility for personal and social change. The process involves both the abandonment of racism and the development of a nonracist White identity. Helms (1999) proposes a model with two phases, each with three levels, called statuses.

## PHASE I: ABANDONMENT OF RACISM

1. *Contact:* The person is color blind about difference and accepts White supremacy. He or she lacks awareness of cultural and institutional racism and of his or her own White privilege. He or she believes that White is not a color. This stage often includes naïve curiosity about or fear of people of color, based on stereotypes learned from friends, family, and the media. These stereotypes represent the framework in use when a person at this stage makes a comment such as, "You don't act like a Black person." Whites whose lives are structured in such a way that they have limited interaction with people of color may remain at this stage indefinitely.

2. *Disintegration:* The person begins to see the consequences of racism and feels conflicted; the breakdown of denial can mean anxiety and psychological pain. He or she begins to think that maybe being White does matter and moves from the bliss of ignorance or lack of awareness to the discomfort of guilt, shame, and sometimes anger at the recognition of his or her own advantage due to being White and acknowledgment of the role of Whites in a racist system. Attempts to reduce discomfort may include denial, withdrawal, and attempts to change other White folks' attitudes toward people of color. For example, a person may begin to notice the racist content of jokes or comments of friends and relatives and try to confront them.

3. *Reintegration:* The person regresses into the dominant ideology as a retreat and has a "bootstrap" perspective about poverty with an "I did it, so can they" attitude. While the person recognizes his or her Whiteness, this state is characterized by a defensive attitude of "So what if I'm White?!" Societal pressure to accept the status quo and a desire to be accepted by one's own racial group may lead the person at this stage to reshape his or her beliefs to be more congruent with an acceptance of racism. The person's guilt and anxiety may be redirected as fear and anger against people of color, who are now blamed as the source of discomfort. It is relatively easy for Whites to become stuck at this stage, particularly if they can avoid interactions with people of color. However, if there is a catalyst for continued self-examination, the

person begins to question his or her previous definition of Whiteness and the justifiability of racism in any form. Since the person's worldview at the reintegration stage tends to be rigid and firmly held, movement out of this stage usually necessitates a personally jarring event, such as a drastic change in racial climate, a racist incident that cannot be simply justified, or a significant relationship with a person who succeeds in breaking through to challenge the person's assumptions.

## PHASE II: DEFINING A NONRACIST IDENTITY

4. *Pseudo-independence:* The person experiences events that trigger insight into racism and induce more understanding of diversity differences while still valuing solutions that support the status quo. The person is abandoning beliefs in White superiority but may still behave in ways that unintentionally perpetuate the system. He or she looks to people of color to help him or her understand racism and often tries to disavow his or her own Whiteness through active affiliation with people of color. The person feels alienated from other Whites who have not yet begun to examine their own racism, yet also feels rejected by people of color who are suspicious of his or her motives.

5. *Immersion/emersion:* The person moves into dealing with his or her Whiteness, privilege, biases, and oppression; this involves undoing distortion and denial. This is a major shift away from focusing on people of color to focusing on understanding racism and on changing oneself. The person seeks to replace racially related myths and stereotypes with accurate information about what it means and has meant to be White in U.S. society. Learning about Whites who have been antiracist allies is a very important part of this process of getting to know that others have found ways to resist racism.

6. *Autonomy:* The person's increased awareness of his or her own Whiteness involves "reduced feelings of guilt, acceptance of one's role in perpetuating racism, and renewed determination to abandon white entitlement" (Helms, 1999, p. 152). The person has internalized a newly defined sense of self as White. The positive feelings associated with this redefinition energize the person's efforts to confront racism and

oppression. Alliances with people of color can be forged more easily at this stage because the person's antiracist behaviors and attitudes are expressed more consistently.

If you are White, the following exercise is aimed at helping you discover or rediscover your feelings about your race.

**REFLECTION EXERCISE 4.6**
**REDISCOVERING MY FEELINGS ABOUT BEING WHITE***

Think back to when you first became truly aware that you were *White*. Close your eyes and imagine yourself back in the situation. Try to feel what you felt at the time. Focus on *yourself* rather than on other people. Write about your experience in your journal.

1. Who was involved in the situation, and what were their races?
2. What happened to you?
3. When that happened, you felt . . .
4. Describe your bodily sensations at the time.
5. What did you do in response to your feelings or bodily sensations?
6. How did you feel about being White when this particular situation was over?
7. What did you learn about being White?

You may want to try this exercise several times, using experiences from different times in your life for analysis.

Refer back to your analyses of yourself. We hope they provided some ideas about how you react daily to being a White person. Review the stages of White racial identity development presented previously and think about where you might be in your own development. Consider keeping a daily diary in which you record your experiences of being consciously White.

*Adapted from Helms (1992, pp. 69–72).

## Multiracial Identity Development

The growing number of individuals who identify as multiracial or multicultural bears particular attention because of the societal pressure to identify as belonging to one racial group; that individuals with multiple racial identities are categorized as having one overriding, monolithic racial identity; and based on the "one drop rule" (Wright, 1994), dominant society classifies African Americans as Black when their parents are Euro-American and African American. Root's (1990, 1992, 1996, 2001) writing highlights how individuals with multiple racial heritage often experience marginalization, prejudice, and discrimination due to society's difficulty in appreciating and accepting an identity based on not one, but multiple ethnic and racial heritages. Her work brings attention to pressures the individual may feel to have a racial identity imposed, subjection to negative stereotyping, and feeling little support to process and understand the meaning for themselves of their racial and social identity. Drawing from the "one drop rule" and Root's (1996) writing, Sue and Sue (2003) point out that any African American heritage ascribes a monolithic African American identity to an individual, based on the what is called *hypodescent.* Hypodescent refers to the myth of a single racial identity and assigning individuals of multiple racial heritages the lowest social power status. Growing attention is being given to the unique tasks of identity development for multiracial people (Kerwin & Ponterotto, 1995; Root, 1992). Although the "one drop rule" brings much attention to a heritage of African American and Euro-American, it is important to recognize that all individuals of multiple ethnic and racial heritages experience the pressures and conflicts of choosing one rather than appreciating all they have inherited.

Tremendous work is required to integrate multiple racial and social heritage, particularly when taking into account the varying degrees of societal legitimization that different groups do or do not enjoy. It falls on the shoulders of each multiracial and multiethnic individual to work through conflicts and validate his or her own background in ways that may not be supported within his or her immediate support network. Society values people from various national and ethnic origins differently, which creates challenges for a person in the process of dealing with the developmental tasks of a multiracial identity. This is particularly the case when racism results in avoidance and invisibility of some aspects of a person's identity. Biracial identity models explore issues such as the possible relegation to marginal membership in one's primary groups (Stonequist, as cited in Kerwin &

Ponterotto, 1995), self esteem, feelings of disloyalty, racism, experiences with society's uncertainty regarding race, and factors that support functioning in more than one culture (Jacobs, 1992; Kerwin & Ponterotto, 1995; Kich, 1992; LaFromboise, Coleman, & Gerton, 1993; Poston, 1990).

If you are multiracial, the following exercise seeks to help you discover or rediscover your feelings about your race.

## REFLECTION EXERCISE 4.7
## REDISCOVERING MY FEELINGS ABOUT BEING MULTIRACIAL[*][†]

Think back to when you first became truly aware that you were *multiracial*. Close your eyes and imagine yourself back in the situation. Try to feel what you felt at the time. Focus on *yourself* rather than on other people. Write about your experience in your journal.

1. Who was involved in the situation, and what were their races[‡]?
2. What happened to you?
3. When that happened, you felt . . .
4. Describe your bodily sensations at the time.
5. What did you do in response to your feelings or bodily sensations?
6. How did you feel about being multiracial when this particular situation was over?
7. What did you learn about being multiracial?

You may want to try this exercise several times, using experiences from different times in your life for analysis.

Refer back to your analyses of yourself. We hope they provided some ideas about how you react daily to being a multicultural person. Review the stages of both Black and White racial identity development presented previously as well as the discussion related to multiracial identity development, and think about where you might be in your own development. Consider keeping a daily diary in which you record your experiences of being consciously multiracial.

---

[*]Adapted from Helms (1992, pp. 69–72).
[†]Multiracial is used to refer to individuals with multiple racial heritages; it is not presumed to be a social identity.
[‡]The term *race* is used in the context of understanding it as a social construct.

# Summary: Racial Identity Development and Cultural Competence

In this chapter, we focused on social identity, particularly as it relates to race and ethnicity, as essential to understanding diversity and commitment to social justice. We maintained that understanding your own racial identity is an essential component of cultural competence.

Three distinct racial identity models were presented that address the developmental dynamics of coming to terms with racism and oppression in society and the internalization of their effects as they work for members of particular racial groups. These models address the internalization of dominant ideological belief systems, realization of an identity based on privilege or marginalization, and a movement toward the formulation of an identity that no longer needs a self-definition that is contingent on having to devalue an "other" as the bearer of socially devalued qualities (e.g., lazy, dirty, immoral, irresponsible, abusive). When you have a wholesome identity, you have the capacity to own characteristics that were by past necessity projected onto others through negative stereotyping. Being free of the distortion that comes from privilege or target status leaves you able to appraise and reject overestimations of self premised on entitlement and privilege, or underestimation of self based on your target status.

As a culturally competent social worker, your awareness of your own racial and social identity and your willingness to confront the issues in your own personal and professional life are a prerequisite for attending to your clients' racial and social identity needs to help them through effective change processes. This means taking time to do the emotional and intellectual work involved in addressing the complex concerns that arise from your own racial and social identity development processes. The rewarding result is gaining a variety of new perspectives about diversity.

The old adage of starting where the client is offers a particularly useful guide for you as you engage in learning about diversity, oppression, and social justice. It is essential to validate your own struggles and intentions. Throughout the process, it is important to suspend judgment of yourself and to remember that this is a lifelong process of integrating the political into the personal. As you explore and analyze your own racial identity development process, you are engaging in work that most people do not have the courage or the proclivity to do. The work is uncomfortable, so it is important to be gentle with yourself and your peers through the process.

# References

Arredondo, P., Toporek, R., Brown, S. P., Jones, J., Locke, D. C., Sanchez, J., et al. (1996). Operationalization of the multicultural competencies. *Journal of Multicultural Counseling and Development, 24,* 42–78.

Berger, P., & Luckman, T. (1966). *The social construction of reality.* New York: Doubleday & Company.

Cross, W. E. (1995). The psychology of nigrescence: Revising the Cross Model. In J. G. Ponterotto, J. M. Casas, L. A. Suzuki, & C. M. Alexander (Eds.), *Handbook of multicultural counseling* (pp. 181–191). Thousand Oaks, CA: Sage.

Hacker, A. (1992). *Two nations: Black and white, separate, hostile, unequal.* New York: Charles Scribner's Sons.

Hardiman, R. (1982). White identity development: A process oriented model for describing the racial consciousness of White Americans. *Dissertations Abstracts International, 43,* 104A (University Microfilms No. 82-10330).

Helms, J. (Ed.). (1990). *Black and white racial identity: Theory, research and practice.* Westport, CT: Greenwood Press.

Helms, J. (1995). An update of Helms's White and people of color racial identity models. In J. G. Ponterotto, J. M. Casas, L. A. Suzuki, & C. M. Alexander (Eds.), *Handbook of multicultural counseling* (pp. 181–191). Thousand Oaks, CA: Sage.

Helms, J. (1999). White racial identity development: Therapeutic implications. In D. Sue & D. Sue (Eds.), *Counseling the culturally different* (3rd ed.). New York: John Wiley & Sons, Inc.

Helms, J. E. (1992). *A race is a nice thing to have.* Topeka, KS: Content Communications.

Highlen, P. S., Reynolds, A. L., Adams, E. M., Hanley, T. C., Myers, L. J., Cox, C., et al. (1988, August 13). *Self-identity developmental model for oppressed people: inclusive model for all?* Paper presented at the American Psychological Association Convention, Atlanta, GA.

Jackson, B., & Hardiman, R. (n.d.). *Social identity development model.* Unpublished manuscript.

Jacobs, J. H. (1992). Identity development in biracial children. In M. P. P. Root (Ed.), *Racially mixed people in America* (pp. 190–206). Newbury Park, CA: Sage.

Keefe, S. (1992). Ethnic identity: The domain of perceptions of and attachment to ethnic groups and cultures. *Human Organizations, 51,* 35–43.

Keefe, S., & Padilla, A. (1987). *Chicano ethnicity.* Albuquerque: University of New Mexico Press.

Kerwin, C., & Ponterotto, J. G. (1995). Biracial identity development: Theory and research. In J. G. Ponterotto, J. M. Casas, L. A. Suzuki, & C. M. Alexander (Eds.), *Handbook of multicultural counseling* (pp. 199–217). Thousand Oaks, CA: Sage.

Kich, G. K. (1992). The developmental process of asserting a biracial, bicultural identity. In M. P. P. Root (Ed.), *Racially mixed people in America* (pp. 304–317). Newbury Park, CA: Sage.

LaFromboise, T., Coleman, H. L. K., & Gerton, J. (1993). Psychological impact of biculturalism: Evidence and theory. *Psychological Bulletin, 114,* 395–412.

Phinney, J. (1990). Ethnic identity in adolescents and adults: Review of research. *Psychological Bulletin, 108*(3), 499–514.

Phinney, J. (1996). When we talk about American ethnic groups, what do we mean? *American Psychologist, 51*(9), 918–927.

Poston, W. S. (1990). The biracial identity development model: A needed addition. *Journal of Counseling and Development, 69,* 152–155.

Robinson, T., & Howard-Hamilton, M. (2000). *The convergence of race, ethnicity and gender.* Columbus, OH: Prentice Hall.

Root, M. P. P. (1990). Resolving "other" status: Identity development of biracial individuals. In L. S. Borwn & M. P. P. Root (Eds.), *Diversity and complexity in feminist therapy* (pp. 185–205). New York: Haworth.

Root, M. P. P. (1992). *Racially mixed people in America.* Thousand Oaks, CA: Sage.

Root, M. P. P. (Ed.). (1996). *The multiracial experience.* Thousand Oaks, CA: Sage.

Root, M. P. P. (2001). Negotiating the margins. In J. G. Ponterotto, J. M. Casas, L. A. Suzuki, & C. M. Alexander (Eds.). *Handbook of multicultural counseling.* Thousand Oaks, CA: Sage.

Sue, D., & Sue, D. (2003). *Counseling the cultural diverse: Theory and practice* (4th ed.). New York: John Wiley & Sons, Inc.

Wright, L. (1994, July 25). One drop of blood. *The New Yorker,* 46–55.

# Chapter Five
# Pulling It All Together:
# A Case Study

Throughout this book the emphasis has been on two professional social work responsibilities that are inextricably linked: providing culturally competent services and promoting social and economic justice. In this chapter we provide opportunities for you to bring these two responsibilities together through a process of applying the book's conceptual framework and key concepts to a case study. It is hoped that, by working with a client situation, this will lead you to 1) develop increased understanding of the patterns, dynamics, and consequences of oppression related to particular clients from historically disadvantaged groups, and 2) gain knowledge and skills to assess, intervene, and promote social and economic justice effectively as a basic element of culturally competent practice. The goal is to help you face the double challenges of understanding societal oppression *and* translating that understanding into actions designed to facilitate social change for social justice.

## Creating a Frame for Work With a Case Study

Before beginning, it is important to summarize briefly the content covered in the first four chapters, as that content will frame the probes you apply to the case study. Chapter 1 began with a vision for social work, followed by a discussion of social justice definitions and a presentation of five contemporary perspectives of social justice. You were encouraged to think critically about your own beliefs and examine them through the lens of promoting social and economic justice for diverse populations as the basis for culturally competent social work practice. Distributive justice theory provides a basis for understanding the complexity of one's notions about what social justice *should be* and the reality of social injustice as it currently exists. The racial contract is most consistent with this book's premise that diversity and social justice are inextricably entwined. Analysis of one's notions about social justice, based on Rawls's (1971) early work, leads to a recognition that the beliefs one holds about social justice are race-, class-, and gender-based. This process highlights the presence of oppression, its dynamics, and how it shows up differently in diverse populations. The racial contract reveals that some people are seen as expendable and undeserving, so they are excluded from the realm of social justice. That is to say, some people are not included in, nor do they benefit from, the social contract. They are vulnerable to the negative labeling placed on those groups with which they identify, and their oppression and exclusion are premised on stereotypes and prejudicial attitudes related to ethnocentrism. A human rights perspective of social justice provides the solution that all people are entitled to the same universal rights, without discrimination.

Chapter 2 provided a context and theoretical foundation for learning processes seeking to transform oppressive and unjust systems into nonoppressive and just alternatives (Gil, 1998). Some persistent issues and obstacles faced on the journey to develop cultural competence were also highlighted. Culturally competent practice involves exposing the ways in which cultural assumptions, frames of reference, and biases within the social work profession influence what social workers think they know about people and their environments and the strategies they adopt with the intention of being helpful. It means examining how knowledge is created, represents power, and is influenced by factors of race, ethnicity, gender, class, ability, and sexual orientation.

In chapter 3, we presented fundamental concepts and issues to provide a foundation for culturally competent social work practice. The beginning point for such a foundation is a focus on racism as the fundamental form of oppression from which other forms of oppression can be understood. Discussion about multiple identities and multiple, intersecting types of oppression illustrated the complex dynamics related to issues of power and privilege. Oppression was characterized by social rather than individual power, institutionalization of norms, and practices and laws that maintain their political and social hold and that are held in place by ideology and violence—both real and threatened. The concept of moral exclusion was presented as a tool for helping to explore beliefs about who is deemed worthy of being treated fairly and justly. Culturally competent social work practice is empowerment-based, supports self-determination, recognizes the multiple levels and dynamics of oppression and racism, and is grounded in and inspired by historical events and actions that have resulted in social change.

Chapter 4 dealt specifically with the concept of social identity as it relates to ethnicity and what is called *race*. One's ethnic and racial identity complements and is inextricably connected to one's understanding of and commitment to social justice, the focus of chapter 1. The stance of this book is that cultural competency requires the integration of diversity and social justice. Thus, the focus is on understanding one's own racial identity as an essential component of cultural competence. Three distinct racial identity models were presented that address the developmental dynamics of coming to terms with racism and oppression in society and the internalization of their effects as they work for members of particular racial groups. These models address the process that begins with internalization of dominant ideological belief systems and realization of an identity based on privilege or marginalization. Such increased awareness moves a person toward the formulation of an identity that does not need a self-definition contingent on the devaluation of an "other." "Other" means those in society who are viewed as bearers of those socially devalued qualities (e.g., lazy, dirty, immoral, irresponsible, abuser) that one rejects in oneself. When you have a wholesome identity, you have the capacity to own characteristics that in the past, due to discomfort, were projected onto others through negative stereotyping. Being free of distortion arising from privilege or target status leaves you able to appraise and reject overestimations of self, premised on entitlement and privilege, or underestimation of self, based on target status. As a culturally competent social worker, awareness of your own racial and social identity and your willingness to confront issues in your own personal and professional life are a prerequisite for attending to your clients' racial and social identity needs to promote and facilitate effective change processes. This means taking time to do the emotional and intellectual work involved in addressing the complex concerns that arise from your own racial and social identity development processes.

This final chapter now moves on to apply the material presented in the first four chapters to a case study. A brief description of the case study is included in the next section. You are asked to imagine that you are the school social worker who is working with Jason and his family. Following the case study, we will walk you through four processes:

1. Dynamics of difference: understanding issues of power and privilege in the situation

2. Racism, prejudice, and discrimination related to power and privilege: understanding oppression in the situation

3. Empowerment practice: setting social justice goals

4. Culturally competent practice: social and racial identity development

The processes will be addressed in separate sections, with each process involving self-reflection as well as client assessment. You are encouraged to engage in the exercises provided, which are suggested as practice procedures that you can use in a variety of case situations.

# Jason:  A Case Study

Jason is 13 years old and lives with his mother, Mary, and her partner of 10 years, Claire. Mary is licensed and employed as a beautician in a local shop and Claire is a schoolteacher, and they consider themselves to be middle class. As an active, personable African American child, Jason got failing marks in the first grade, yet was passed on to second grade. When his mother asked how he could be promoted if he hadn't learned first grade work, she was told the school needed the room for new first graders. When his mother's partner, Claire, who is White and a schoolteacher in Jason's school, complained about the situation, she was told that they only deal with family members. Even though Claire informed them that she had been a significant mother figure for Jason since he was 3 years old, she was told that school policy requires that they deal only with the child's parents.

Although Mary and Claire have a long-term, stable relationship, they are unable to marry, so Jason and Mary are deprived of health benefits through Claire's work that would cover some of Jason's health (mental and physical) needs. Jason has never been able to keep up in school and talks about dropping out as soon as he can. Outbursts between him and other students often result in his being singled out and penalized by the teacher, with lesser consequences for the other students. He has begun experimenting with alcohol and other drugs.

Jason's father, who was married to his mother for two years, is an addict who has been imprisoned three times for various charges, including breaking and entering, armed robbery, and resisting arrest. During his last arrest, he was subjected to a brutal beating by the police who justified it on the grounds that he was acting bizarrely and reaching for a weapon. While he denies being armed, he accepted a plea bargain on the advice of his court-appointed attorney and is currently serving a prison sentence. Jason hears from his father sporadically, and his mother worries that her ex-husband is a bad influence on the boy.

Jason's mother arranged to have him tested and he was diagnosed with attention deficit disorder (ADD) and dyslexia, among other learning disabilities, and depression. He is failing in school, spends most of his time at home watching television, and sleeps a lot.

Jason's family and their circle of friends provide him with strong support and a loving home, but his struggles are causing them considerable concern at this critical stage in his life. They have turned to the school social worker for help.

# I. Dynamics of Difference: Understanding Issues of Power and Privilege in the Situation

Imagine throughout the rest of this chapter that you are the school social worker who is assigned to work with Jason and his family. In this section, you are encouraged to engage in several self-reflection and assessment exercises related to difference in the situation to understand issues of power and privilege as they affect your work with the family.

The social work principle of "starting where the client is" is applied by suggesting that you first "start with where you are as the social worker." It is important to identify any personal issues and obstacles that might interfere with effective practice. As we pointed out in chapter 1, fear and anger are often related to difference and cultural diversity and are rooted in the secret of privilege—White privilege, male privilege, heterosexual privilege. Cultural diversity is a key issue in Jason's situation: Jason and his mother and father are African American; Jason's mother, Mary, is either a lesbian or bisexual and she is in a long-term relationship with a White woman, Claire. Also, Jason has been diagnosed with disabilities that include ADD, dyslexia, and depression. Examine your own thoughts and feelings related to issues of diversity as represented by Jason, his mother, and her partner by doing the following reflection exercise.

## REFLECTION EXERCISE 5.1  ISSUES OF DIFFERENCE IN THE CASE STUDY

1. Take a moment to consider all the issues of diversity in the case study. List all the elements related to "difference" and/or cultural diversity that are represented.
2. Write down all the ways Jason and his family are similar to you and your family. For each point of similarity, write down all your thoughts and feelings about those similarities.
3. Write down all the ways Jason and his family are different from you and your family. For each point of difference, write down all your thoughts and feelings about those differences.
4. Now look at your two lists of thoughts and feelings, those related to similarities and those related to differences. Which of them do you think represent possible strengths in your work with this family? Which of them do you think represent possible obstacles or barriers?
5. How can you build on the strengths? What do you need to do to address the potential obstacles?
6. Whom and what can you turn to for help in addressing the obstacles? Develop a plan for building on the strengths and overcoming the obstacles.

As you explored your thoughts and feelings in the above exercise, you may have identified points of discomfort. It is particularly important to stay with that discomfort and explore it further. As we maintained in chapter 3, an obstacle to learning about diversity is often fear and anger that are rooted in the secret of unmerited privilege that comes with being a member of a dominant group. Unearned privileges are granted by a system that advantages some people due to race, gender, sexual orientation, and ability, while it disadvantages others. Unearned privileges include the daily ways in which privilege makes some people comfortable or powerful and provides supports, assets, approval, and rewards to those who are members of the privileged group (McIntosh, 1995).

The case of Jason and his family illustrates how the concept of privilege works. Jason, who is African American and has disabilities, is denied privileges that are conferred on those who are White and have no disabilities. Mary, Jason's mother, is denied privileges that are conferred on those who are White, male, and heterosexual. Claire, Mary's partner, is denied privileges that are conferred on those who are male and heterosexual, while she is granted privileges that are conferred on those who are White. It is important that the social worker understand the role of privilege and power in the lives of Jason, Mary, and Claire. Further, to deeply understand the role of privilege in their lives, the social worker must first look at his or her own privilege or lack of privilege related to race, gender, sexual orientation, and ability. To that end, you are encouraged to do the following reflection exercise.

# II. Racism, Prejudice, and Discrimination, Related to Power and Privilege: Understanding Oppression in the Situation

As members of a middle-income, African American family, with a mother and her partner in a lesbian relationship, and a father who has an addiction and a prison history, this family is vulnerable to prejudice, discrimination, and institutional racism. Racism is unique in that it represents societal belief patterns that are seen as "normal." Unlike prejudice and discrimination,

**REFLECTION EXERCISE 5.2**
**UNPACKING/PACKING YOUR PRIVILEGES AS THE SOCIAL WORKER**

1. List characteristics associated with your identity related to race, gender, sexual orientation, and ability. In other words, are you White or a person of color? Male or female? Heterosexual or gay/lesbian/bisexual/transgender? A person with or without a disability?
2. Go back to chapter 2 and review the work you did in Reflection Exercises 2.2, 2.3, and 2.4 related to race privilege, gender privilege, and heterosexual privilege. If you did not do those exercises, you are encouraged to do so now.
3. How do you feel about having and benefiting from the privileges that have been conferred on you? How do you feel about not having privileges when they have been denied?
4. How is your having or not having privilege based on race, gender, sexual orientation, and ability similar to or different from Jason and his family?
5. What are your thoughts and feelings about the similarities and differences in your privileges compared to those of Jason and his family?
6. What are the points of discomfort that you feel related to privilege and working with this family?
7. What can you do to address the potential obstacles in working with Jason and his family related to privilege and power? Develop a plan for addressing the discomfort or potential obstacles.

which assume mal intent, racism's institutional characteristics allow its practice even among the "well intentioned" (Gaertner & Dovidio, 1981). Earlier exercises explored how the relationship between one's cultural identification(s) and dominant cultural values results in societal validation and affirmation and/or invisibility and denial. Societal validation or denial is based on one's membership in a group that is the target of oppression (i.e., racism, classism, sexism, heterosexism).

You will now have an opportunity to examine prejudice, discrimination, and racism in the life of Jason's family by exploring elements of his life as well as your own. Before you examine prejudice, discrimination, and racism, we encourage you to do the following reflection exercise to probe into images that come to your mind in regard to the vignette and your own life and, thus, to promote reflection about and heighten awareness of both life experiences. This is the first of several exercises that build on one another by inquiring about your perceptions about the vignette and simultaneously asking you to apply the probes to yourself.

**REFLECTION EXERCISE 5.3A**
**DOMINANT CULTURE VERSUS MARGINALIZED CULTURE**

This exercise builds on Classroom Exercise 3.2 in chapter 3. In the two columns below, respond to the following points about Jason's family and your family. You are asked to use your imagination regarding associations that come to mind based on the available profile of Jason's family. If you expect there might not be any activities, say so and describe your rationale. When you finish this exercise, move on to Exercise 5.3b.

**Jason's Family**                    **My Family**

1. Describe a representative family meal, who is present, and the factors you perceive to influence the choice of food, location, and other characteristics.

2. Describe a special family event and factors you perceive as influencing its characteristics (e.g., location, participants, props/artifacts) and activities

3. Describe a spiritual/religious event, its location, and participants you might expect Jason and his family to interact with; be specific regarding the relationship of participants to Jason as well as the participants in your life example.

|  |  |
|---|---|
|  |  |

4. Describe characteristics of a workplace where Jason's mothers could be employed and one where you currently work, have worked in, or could work in. Comment on the nature of the working relationships and psychological climate (e.g., comfort level, tensions).

|  |  |
|---|---|
|  |  |

5. Describe a couple of recreational and/or leisure activities, that is, activities you enjoy. Identify the resources needed to engage in these activities.

| a.<br><br>b. | a.<br><br>b. |
|---|---|

## REFLECTION EXERCISE 5.3B
## DOMINANT CULTURE VERSUS MARGINALIZED CULTURE

Review your responses to the five queries in part A of this exercise and reflect on the following:

- What types of differences stand out between your life experiences and those you wrote down about Jason's family? Be specific. Do the differences you imagine appear to be related totally to choice and beliefs or are other factors at play? What might those factors be?

**REFLECTION EXERCISE 5.3B**
**DOMINANT CULTURE VERSUS MARGINALIZED CULTURE (continued)**

•What types of similarities stand out for you? What are your thoughts about the implications of these similarities?

•What stereotypes and prejudices did you become aware of in relation to Jason and his family's profile as you looked at the images you imagined about them?

•When you wrote down your images of Jason's family, what did you base them on? What additional information do you need to get from Jason's family?

The next activity is intended to shift your attention to another layer of Jason and his family's experiences as they relate to low social power and negative societal stereotypes. The exercise first examines individual behavioral dynamics (i.e., prejudice, discrimination) and then shifts to institutional dynamics (i.e., racism). Although behavioral and institutional phenomena may, and often do, overlap, the decisively powerful element that compromises and complicates people's lives is when prejudice and discrimination occur in a context of institutional racism. More important, the intersection of racism and classism determine the extent and ways that racism affects one's life.

**REFLECTION EXERCISE 5.4**
**DISTINGUISHING AMONG PREJUDICE, DISCRIMINATION, AND RACISM**

1. Identify negative stereotypes that come to mind about Jason and his family. Address these stereotypes based on each of the following: racism, classism, sexism, heterosexism, and ableism.

2. Now draw a map or picture of individuals, groups, and organizations that are in *your* life space. The picture should show those with whom you are most intimate, those who are closest to you.

3. On your map, circle in color those individuals, groups, and organizations that have articulated or might openly articulate *prejudices* based on those stereotypes identified in #1 related to Jason's family. Provide examples.

4. Circle in a different color those individuals, groups, and organizations in your life space that have engaged in or could engage in *discriminatory actions* based on the stereotypes identified in #1 (e.g., through exclusion, name-calling, harassment, physical assault). Give some examples.

5. Consider how *institutional racism* has affected or could affect Jason and his family. What examples come to mind of "business as usual" school or organizational practices that create limits on Jason based on race, without intentionally singling him out. How are these examples different from the discriminatory actions you identified in #4?

6. Describe policy or program directives that could create obstacles that would interfere with this family's well-being and healthy functioning.

7. How might Jason's family's experiences have been different if his mother had a graduate degree and achieved some degree of recognition for her competence? If she were White? If she were heterosexual? Be specific.

The next exercise continues to examine the role of racism by delving further into dimensions of racism and oppression that are undergirded by racism's institutional nature. These dimensions are invisibility, moral exclusion, and conflicts associated with having multiple social identities. A common element of oppression is the invisibility endured by the individuals in groups that are oppressed. When society devalues and renders invisible aspects of a person's identity, this inevitably leads to individuals undervaluing and making invisible to themselves substantive parts of their own origins and history. An example of this can be a lack of role models who share one's identity.

The concept of moral exclusion explains how exclusionary behavior is promoted and maintained on an interpersonal level through a process of placing those who are different from oneself or one's group outside the boundaries of fair treatment by invoking assumptions about who deserves just treatment and who should enjoy society's benefits. For example, Jason's mother and her partner represent gay/lesbian/bisexual/transgender persons who have been and are excluded from the norms and values of social justice. Reflection Exercise 5.5 helps you work with the concepts of invisibility, moral exclusion, and the notion of individual and social power as they relate to you and your family and to Jason and his family.

---

**REFLECTION EXERCISE 5.5**
**ELEMENTS OF OPPRESSION: INVISIBILITY, MORAL EXCLUSION, INTERSECTIONS; PSYCHOLOGICAL VERSUS SOCIAL POWER**

Respond to the following points in relation to Jason and his family and your family:

### Jason and His Family

1. Given impressions that you have of Jason's culture and life experiences, what images come to mind regarding media characters, heroes, and contemporary and historical role models whom he would admire? Consider both genders and all ethnic/racial groups.
2. In relation to "moral exclusion," where morality is invoked for the purpose of exclusion, what negative judgments could be made about Jason and his family based on "moral" judgments?
3. What strengths do you see in Jason, his mother, and her partner that might be invisible to others?
4. What type of individual power do you see Jason and his family having? Describe some examples of how Jason, his mother, and her partner have or could exercise their individual power.

5. Describe the social power (low, high) that Jason and his family have. What are some examples and settings where social power is exemplified in their lives?

### Me and My Family

1. Identify media characters, heroes (both genders), and contemporary and historical role models who currently have a place of prominence in your life. Consider both genders and all ethnic/racial groups.

2. What assumptions do you and your family make about values that are held by the dominant cultural group? Are the values you hold the same as those held by individuals and families such as Jason's? Be specific.

3. What aspects of your background and life experiences do you see as strengths that you identify with and enjoy having people know about you?

4. Describe the individual power that you feel you have and the people (e.g., family, friends, intimates, co-workers/colleagues, etc.) with whom you exercise that power.

5. Describe the social power (low, high) that you have. Be specific regarding the basis (source) of that power and where you exercise it (e.g., as a family member, with your church group, as a college student, in your community, etc.).

Issues related to multiple identities further complicate the picture when looking at Jason and his family. Individual conditions of oppression within family members converge between aspects of their experience where they are the targets of oppression (e.g., Jason and his mother being African American, Jason being a person with disabilities, Mary and Claire being lesbian or bisexual) and other aspects of their experience as privileged (e.g., Claire being White, the family being middle income). Reflection Exercise 5.6 provides an opportunity for you to delve further into dimensions of racism and oppression related to multiple social identities.

**REFLECTION EXERCISE 5.6  MULTIPLE SOCIAL IDENTITIES**

### Jason and His Family

1. Make a list of the social identities (based on background, life experience, interests, e.g., African American, middle income, student, etc.) with which you imagine Jason would identify.
2. What aspects of Jason and his family's identifications and experiences might they be inclined to downplay or ignore due to the potential for denigration of these qualities? What do you think accounts for the reality that these unique aspects of Jason and his family's life are not recognized or considered by those who are different from them?
3. Where do you think Jason and his family find support for all the parts and facets of their identity?
4. In light of social work practice placing value on affirming the multiple social identities individuals have, what considerations would you find helpful in preparing to work with Jason and his family? For you, what does meeting the "client where the client is at" imply in working with Jason and his family?

### Me and My Family

1. List the various aspects of your social identity (identifications) related to your background, experiences, and interests.
2. Identify those aspects of your identity about which you feel some discomfort or ambivalence that you downplay or ignore with others who do not know you.
3. Where do find support for all the parts and facets of your identity that represent, in total, who you are? Give examples.

As you explored the probes about multiple social identities in the preceding exercise, you may have found yourself reflecting on aspects of Jason and his family's experiences that are often minimized or ignored, even though they are perceptible. You also may have found yourself considering aspects of each of your experiences that make both you and Jason and his family more complex persons than others recognize. The next exercise moves into the domain of oppression and culturally competent practice. This activity is a first step toward additional cultural competency exercises presented later in relation to social and racial identity.

---

**REFLECTION EXERCISE 5.7**
**OPPRESSION CONCEPTS AND CULTURALLY COMPETENT PRACTICE**

1. Given the presence of various levels of oppression (prejudice, discrimination, institutional racism), what implications do these have for how you will approach and work with Jason and his family? What dynamics might arise in relation to their perceptions of you as a representative of a profession? An organization? In light of your ethnic/race, class profile, sexual orientation?

2. If you were to approach working with these individuals and this family system grounded in knowledge of the historical events that are relevant to them, what would you hypothesize these meaningful events might be? It may help to refer to Charts 3.1 and 3.2 in chapter 3 as you think about this question.

3. Given that social work practice is empowerment-based and supports self-determination, what interventions with Jason and his family, on a micro, meso, and macro level, would embody these professional values? Give examples of interventions at each level.

4. A social change approach is implemented both at the level of your practice with individuals and families and with advocacy work at community and organizational levels. What are some examples of social change efforts that you might consider as a focus of your direct services to Jason, his mother, and the family as a whole?

5. What are some examples of social change efforts relevant to Jason's family's concerns that you could engage in as a professional on community, organizational, and institutional levels?

# III. Empowerment Practice: Setting Social Justice Goals

Throughout this book we have maintained that a commitment to promoting social justice for diverse individuals and populations is the foundation of culturally competent social work practice. Promoting social justice requires practice that is empowerment-based. It is critical that culturally competent social workers *themselves* feel empowered to advocate for social justice if they want to be able to facilitate the empowerment of diverse clients to advocate for themselves. Thus, this section on empowerment practice for social justice begins with a reflection exercise that addresses your own sense of empowerment and implications for your work with Jason and his family.

## REFLECTION EXERCISE 5.8  EMPOWERMENT PRACTICE

1. Empowerment concepts suggest that you as a professional must first feel empowered to facilitate the empowerment of others. How do you see yourself as an empowered person? Describe qualities about yourself that reflect empowerment. Where you feel ambivalence, describe what you think you need to feel more empowered. Address your experiences on all three levels of personal, interpersonal, and political power as you reflect on how you see yourself as empowered or disempowered.

2. Based on your reflections above, what goals might you set for yourself to move toward a stronger sense of empowerment? Be specific and realistic in setting your goals.

3. Empowerment practice must be founded on your belief in the capacity of individuals and environments to change. Reflect on Jason's situation and what you would look for (in Jason, his mother, her partner, the family system, school, community, etc.) as a basis for change.

4. Apply the three levels of empowerment (personal, interpersonal, political) to Jason's mother. What issues do you think might interfere with her feeling empowered on these three levels. What might she need to feel empowered on all three levels? Do the same for Jason.

Setting social justice goals as a part of culturally competent practice requires critical thinking about your own beliefs about social justice and an examination of those beliefs through the lens of promoting social and economic justice for diverse populations. In chapter 1 we presented three types of social justice—distributive, legal, and commutative—and five contemporary perspectives of distributive social justice. We suggest that you review the content in that chapter and then complete the following reflection exercise. This exercise is intended to help you to apply the social justice concepts to Jason's situation as a way to think through issues of injustice as a normal part of a case assessment.

## REFLECTION EXERCISE 5.9
## DIVERSITY PRACTICE FOR SOCIAL JUSTICE

Consider Jason and his family's needs in relation to the following social justice concerns and your thoughts about what is just and fair:

1. Consider the three types of social justice (distributive, legal, and commutative) presented in chapter 1. Briefly summarize the distinctions among the three before moving on to apply them to the following questions.
2. When you consider Jason's experiences in first grade, his long-standing academic struggles, the school's response to his mother's partner, and the circumstances involved in his father's last arrest, what social justice issues come to mind?
3. Specifically, when Jason was passed from the first grade to the second without having mastered the first grade content, what social justice issues do you see present, if any? Present your rationale.
4. Consider the five theories of *distributive justice* (utilitarian, libertarian, egalitarian, racial contract, human rights) in chapter 3. Apply these to Jason's situation. How would each of these support or detract from the interests, quality of life, and justice concerns of Jason and his family?
5. In regard to distributive justice, what do you feel society owes Jason? To move him on with his cohorts so he does not become marginalized at a vulnerable age? To keep him in first grade so he learns foundational knowledge? Providing first grade

REFLECTION EXERCISE 5.9
**DIVERSITY PRACTICE FOR SOCIAL JUSTICE (continued)**

    curriculum and staff that will address his unique learning needs and prepare him for second grade? Provide services for his ADD, depression? Be specific and present your rationale.

6. Think more about the other social justice issues in this situation. For example, what are the issues related to Jason's mother and her partner? To Jason's father?

7. In a preliminary way, consider which social justice issues you would address first with this family. Be specific. What interventions would you explore in relation to each issue?

8. What strengths do you have that will be helpful in this situation? What strengths does the family have? What barriers do you and the family need to overcome?

# IV. Culturally Competent Practice: Social and Racial Identity Development

One's racial and ethnic identity complements and is inextricably connected to one's understanding of and commitment to social justice. In this section, the focus is on helping you to apply what you have learned about social identity in relation to oppression and racism in society to your work with Jason and his family. Social identity refers to two aspects: communality, which occurs through cultural identification and reference groups that speak to your interests, and social power, an aspect of identity that is affected by oppression regardless of whether you benefit from privilege or are a target of oppression. Review the discussion on pages 107–110 about three distinct dimensions of life experiences that combine and interact in the process of forming one's social identity (Arredondo et al., 1996). The "A" dimension represents characteristics that individuals are born into and over which they have the least control. Each "A" dimension—whether age/developmental issues, culture, ethnicity, gender, language, disability, sexual orientation, or socioeconomic class—is the basis of either oppression or privilege. This dimension can be used to assess a client's social power position based on multiple identities. The "B" dimension represents the resources that are developed in one's lifetime and is seen as resulting from the interactions between what individuals are born with (the "A" dimension) and the sociopolitical contexts of their lives (the "C" dimension). For those who experience oppression and racism, the "A" dimension is the most powerful. It is helpful for social workers to bring with them their own awareness of themselves about the three dimensions and the implications of who they are and apply it in relation to their client's identity. The dimensions can be a useful tool for assessing client situations, as is illustrated in the next exercise. Table 4.1 in chapter 4 summarizes the three dimensions; refer to it as you do Reflection Exercise 5.10.

## REFLECTION EXERCISE 5.10
## SOCIAL IDENTITY DIMENSIONS IN THE CASE OF JASON AND HIS FAMILY

1. Review your responses to Reflection Exercise 4.4 in chapter 4. If you did not complete that exercise, do so now before applying the exercise to Jason's family.
2. Using Table 4.1 in chapter 4 as your guide, list all of the characteristics with which Jason was born ("A" dimension). Which of these characteristics result in benefits of privilege for him? Which of them result in negative stereotypes and his being a target of oppression? What further information do you need to complete an assessment of Jason on this dimension?
3. List the resources that Jason may have developed for himself up to this point in his life and make a separate list of the resources he might seek in the future ("B" dimension). If you think he doesn't have an image of the future, say that, too.
   •Next to each item on Jason's possible list of hopes and

REFLECTION EXERCISE 5.10
**SOCIAL IDENTITY DIMENSIONS IN THE CASE OF JASON AND HIS FAMILY (continued)**

intentions, identify factors (parents, family, teachers, media, friends) that may have had a role in shaping those hopes and intentions.

•What further information do you need to gather to complete an assessment of Jason on this dimension?

4. Make a list of the different events in the sociopolitical context of Jason's life so far ("C" dimension). What do you think might be in his immediate or more remote environment that influences how he sees himself, his present options, and his future? Respond to any of the factors identified in Table 4.1 for "C" dimension and/or identify others that might not be described there. What further information do you need to gather to complete an assessment of Jason on the "C" dimension?

5. Reflect on how the interactions between the characteristics with which Jason was born ("A") and the sociopolitical context in which he lives ("C") have influenced the resources he has developed for himself and his hopes for the future ("B").

6. Repeat #2–#5 in relation to Jason's mother and then her partner, Claire.

Racial identity concepts propose that racism is a normative experience when one grows up in a society characterized by racist values, that is, becoming aware of societal norms and expectations. A social justice approach in social work practice with diverse clients involves taking responsibility for how you have been affected by racism to undo distortions of others and yourself (e.g., having privileged or "other" status). It is important for you to consider how your life experiences influence your view of Jason, his mother, and her partner. It is particularly important to identify what negative stereotypes you invoke when you reflect on their

**REFLECTION EXERCISE 5.11**
**SOCIAL IDENTITY DIMENSIONS AND STEREOTYPES**

Now that you have completed Reflection Exercise 5.10, you should have a picture of yourself and Jason, his mother, and her partner on the three dimensions of identity. The following questions seek to develop consciousness of the influence of social identity on your practice.

1. Step back and compare your identity profile on the three dimensions with Jason's profile. What do you and Jason have in common in relation to life experiences? How are your life experiences different?
2. As you look at Jason's "A" dimension in particular, what stereotypes might you see as you consider Jason's characteristics?
3. In thinking about establishing a helping relationship with Jason and reflecting on the similarities and differences in your life experiences, make a list of things you need to learn about Jason to understand life from his identity experience as much as possible. What issues within yourself related to your own social identity do you need to attend to?
4. Repeat #1–#3 in relation to Jason's mother.
5. Repeat #1–#3 in relation to Jason's mother's partner, Claire.

characteristics. Reflection Exercise 5.11 allows you to develop a conscious approach to social identity influences as you work with Jason and his family.

Understanding your own racial identity is an essential component of cultural competence. Social workers need to go through a developmental process to come to terms with racism and oppression in society and the internalization of their effects on their work with clients. Reflection Exercise 5.12 asks you to explore your own development on a deeper level and in relation to Jason and his family.

**REFLECTION EXERCISE 5.12**
**RACIAL AND SOCIAL IDENTITY AS A FOUNDATION FOR CULTURALLY COMPETENT PRACTICE**

1. Racial identity concepts suggest that on a behavioral level, racism is maintained by disowning your own negative, socially unacceptable qualities by projecting them onto the "other," that is, marginalized groups such as African Americans and gay/lesbian/bisexual/transgender individuals. What qualities come to mind that, on a societal level, are projected onto individuals like Jason, his mother and her partner, and his father? How realistic do you think these stereotypes are in relation to capturing the complexity of their lives? Explain your rationale.
2. Identify two or three aspects of the case vignette that can be framed within an empowerment perspective. Be specific.
3. What do your responses to the above two questions suggest about how you would appraise where you are in your work of undoing dominant culture ideological values? What do you feel you have recognized in yourself and are in the process of working on? What do you see ahead of you in your emotional work?
4. Review the racial identity models for African Americans, ethnic Whites, and multiracial individuals on in chapter 4 (pages 115–123). Consider the developmental stages that relate to your ethnic/racial identity and think about where you might be in your development and how that might affect your work with Jason and his family.

# Summary and Conclusion

In this chapter, we applied the key concepts and understandings that were presented in the first four chapters to a case study. The goal in working with the client situation was twofold: 1) to increase your understanding of the patterns, dynamics, and consequences of oppression related to diverse clients, and 2) to increase your knowledge and skills to effectively assess, intervene, and promote social and economic justice as a basic element of culturally competent practice. To achieve that goal, the concepts and principles were consciously applied to Jason and his family and to you as the hypothetical social worker. By focusing on both sides of the helping equation, the client and the social worker, our intent has been to emphasize the impact of the personal experiences, values, beliefs, and feelings of all parties in the helping relationship. This is based on a belief that there are significant obstacles and issues on the journey to cultural competence, many of which are related to feelings of fear and anger related to diversity and social justice issues, and that facing these barriers requires consciousness, openness, and honesty.

This chapter and the book end by reiterating the two inextricably linked responsibilities of social workers: to provide culturally competent services and to promote social and economic justice. A primary premise of this book has been that culturally competent social work involves effective interventions with diverse clients, coupled with a commitment to promote social justice. Our goal has been to help you develop knowledge, understanding, and awareness skills that facilitate your facing the double challenges of understanding societal oppression *and* translating that understanding into actions designed to facilitate social change for social justice. The challenges are daunting. We have presented several concepts that may have raised challenging questions for you. Learning about diversity and oppression involves questioning assumptions and exploring alternative ideas, thus the process can be not only difficult, it can also be emotionally explosive at times. Developing cultural competence is a lifelong journey that requires patience and gentleness—both with oneself and with others. We hope this book has played a challenging and positive role on your journey.

# References

Arrendondo, P., Toporek, R., Brown, S. P., Jones, J., Locke, D. C., Sanchez, J., & Stadler, H. (1996). Operationalization of the multicultural competencies. *Journal of Multicultural Counseling and Development, 24,* 42–78

Gaertner, S. L., & Dovidio, J. F. (1981). Racism among the well intentioned. In

E. Clausen & J. Bermingham (Eds.), *Pluralism, racism and public policy: The search for equality* (pp. 145–159). New York: Macmillan.

Gil, D. (1998). *Confronting injustice and oppression: Concepts and strategies for social workers.* New York: Columbia University Press.

McIntosh, P. (1995). White privilege and male privilege: A personal account of coming to see correspondences through work in women's studies. In M. L. Anderson & P. H. Collins, *Race, class, and gender: An Anthology* (pp. 76–87). New York: Wadsworth.

Rawls, J. (1971). *A theory of justice.* Cambridge, MA: Harvard University Press.

# About the Authors

Betty Garcia, PhD, is a professor at California State University, Fresno, and formerly taught at Simmons College School of Social Work in Boston.

Dorothy Van Soest, PhD, is professor and dean emeritus at the University of Washington School of Social Work in Seattle and former professor and associate dean of social work at The University of Texas at Austin.

Drs. Garcia and Van Soest are authors of the companion book to this text, *Diversity Education for Social Justice: Mastering Teaching Skills,* as well as numerous other publications related to social justice and diversity in social work education.

# Index